MICROCOMPUTER PRIMER

by

**Mitchell Waite
and Michael Pardee**

Howard W. Sams & Co., Inc.
4300 WEST 62ND ST. INDIANAPOLIS, INDIANA 46268 USA

International Standard Book Number: 0-672-21404-0
Library of Congress Catalog Card Number: 76-42879

Printed in the United States of America.

Preface

Until recently, few people have had the opportunity to really get involved with computer hardware and software. However, with the development of the complex integrated circuitry called *microprocessors*, relatively inexpensive, high-quality computers have been brought within financial reach of almost anyone. These small computers, or *microcomputers*, are finding applications not only in business, technology, and industry, but also in the home as versatile recreational devices. Within a few years all kinds of modern appliances and facilities will be operated in conjunction with microcomputers. Obviously, the need for education in microcomputers will be even greater then than it is now.

As the title implies, this is a book of the basic principles of microcomputers. Only the most common characteristics of microcomputers have been covered, in order to keep the book to a reasonable size. The first chapter is simply a brief introduction to microcomputers. Chapter 2, "Basic Computer Concepts," and Chapter 4, "Programming," deal with what happens within the microcomputer from a logical standpoint, which the user should know. Chapter 3, "Hardware," presupposes a working knowledge of electronics and of digital logic circuits; it discusses the electronics behind the logical operations that the microcomputer performs. Appendix A, "Number Systems," will be useful to those who have never been exposed to number systems other than the decimal. Appendix B, "Memories," surveys a variety of microcomputer memories now available.

The authors sincerely hope this book will provide the beginner with sufficient understanding to confidently tackle whichever particular microcomputer he or she selects.

MITCHELL WAITE
MICHAEL PARDEE

Acknowledgments

The authors would like to thank Bob Gumpertz, for his imaginative drawings, which greatly enhance the book. Thanks also go to Barbara Pardee, who provided many hours of typing, as well as had extreme patience with the authors.

For consultation, photographs, and literature, the authors pay their respects to the following individuals:

JERRY MOSELEY, Design Engineer for Digital Telephone Systems, for his contribution to the memory section and his unique drawings.

DON MCLAUGHLIN, Vice President of Engineering, MOS Technology, Inc., for KIM-1 microcomputer boards.

FLOYD HILL, Vice President of Marketing, Vector Electronic Co., for microprocessor packaging samples, breadboards, cages, and wire-wrap tools.

BARNEY HORDOS, Microcomputer System Engineer, National Semiconductor Corp., for SC/MP design information.

HASH PATEL, Microprocessor Marketing Manager, National Semiconductor Corp., for SC/MP microprocessor samples and memory samples.

JOHN KANE, Hewlett-Packard, for LSI calculator photographs.

DICK VUILLEQUEZ, Vice President of Sales, EL Instruments, Inc., for *Bug Books*, microprocessor learning tools, and study systems.

DIANNE ROSS, Marketing Manager, Intel Corp., for microcomputer boards and chip photographs.

CHUCK CHECK, Sales Manager, Prolog Corp., for PROM programmers and logic board photographs.

R. L. AMBURN, Advertising Manager, Pneutronics Division, Gardner-Denver Co., for Wire-Wrap gun photographs.

Contents

APPENDIX A

APPENDIX B

chapter **1**

PERSPECTIVES

Few technological developments have affected us as much as the computer. Perhaps only the automobile could come close to being compared with the computer, considering the latter's impact on our daily lives. The evolution of the computer in the last ten years has been even more rapid than was first expected. We had just become used to seeing the computer as a room full of hard-working tape drives and flashing lights when we were told that state-of-the-art electronics had put a computer on a chip! Just how far this technology will continue to evolve seems beyond our comprehension.

For now, we will discuss some questions regarding the microcomputer, on a general level. We will begin with the most basic question of all:

WHAT IS A MICROCOMPUTER?

"Microcomputer" is the name given to a computer that utilizes an integrated-circuit processor. As we shall discover, the processor is the heart of any computer. Consisting of several different types of electronic circuits, the processor controls the overall operation of the computer. A *microprocessor* is a processor that is contained on one IC chip.

There is, however, more to a computer than simply a processor. As we shall learn, other components are also necessary to make a microprocessor behave like a computer.

WHERE DID MICROPROCESSORS COME FROM?

The early electronic computers were developed at a time in history when the vacuum tube was the prevalent electronic device. Although faster than relays, vacuum tubes had one major drawback. They operated on the principle of "burning themselves out," requiring significant amounts of power in the process. Early computers occupied entire buildings, and demanded heavy-duty cooling apparatus to keep the operating temperature within the specified tolerance.

The arrival of the transistor in the electronics world can be hailed as the turning point in the design of many electronic devices, including the computer. Being an obviously superior replacement for the vacuum tube, the transistor was quickly incorporated into the design of the computer. This led to faster, smaller, and cooler computers. However, computers were still composed of discrete parts. Transistors, diodes, resistors, and capacitors were connected together on printed-circuit boards, and plugged into their respective sockets within the computer.

A few years later, the technology developed that allowed us to build solid-state devices containing several components, all on the same "chip." This was an excellent development for the computer industry, since the large number of switching circuits formerly constructed from discrete components could now be found in a few "integrated circuits." These ICs became the foundation for the pocket calculator. In less than two years the price for an 8-digit electronic calculator was cut in half. The evolution of solid-state technology skyrocketed as

more and more types of integrated-circuit devices became available. The inevitable combining of the computer circuits into one IC chip was to produce the first of the so-called microprocessors in the early 1970s.

WHAT ARE THEY CAPABLE OF DOING?

The first of the microprocessors was not really what you would call a computer. It was programmable, however, within a limited range, and therefore had all the attributes of the larger machines. Within one year these first models were already obsoleted by the development of even more sophisticated versions of microprocessors. The present-day microprocessor is quite capable of being used as the heart of a

general-purpose computing system. The fact that it is entirely self-contained is of little consequence to the programmer, but it means ease of maintenance and repair.

Aside from the general-purpose computing type application, the microcomputer lends itself to many special types of processing. Its physical size will allow it to be included within some other machine, without much physical modification. The continuing decrease in microcomputer cost will lead to many consumer applications which until now have been unrealistic in terms of expense. In short, the world had better get ready for the onrush of the microcomputer. For as sure as $E = IR$, the microcomputer will find its way into the everyday lives of most of us.

HOW HARD IS IT TO GET INTO MICROCOMPUTING?

If you are thinking that you would like to "play around" with a microcomputer, there are certainly many opportunities to do so. Several companies manufacture kits for computers based on some particular chip, and there are also preassembled computers available at a higher price. Of course, the really enterprising experimenters can buy the chips that they will need, and design their own pc boards and enclosures.

The cost of the hardware necessary to build a microcomputer has consistently decreased. Although the first chips were quite expensive, many manufacturers are "getting it together" and the cost has come into the reach of experimenters' budgets. This trend will probably level off at some average amount, and the other components of the computer (memory, I/O devices, etc.) will begin to decrease in price. It's the old principle of supply and demand, for sure.

At this point, the programming of the computer is by far the most significant factor. The hardware can be procured and wired into the correct configuration, but experimenters will most likely have to write their own programs. Ideally, the manufacturer should provide the programs necessary to accomplish whatever the desired processing goal might be. This is not the case, however, and computer experimenters will

spend many hours deeply engrossed in puzzle-solving–type thinking.

WHAT DO I DO WITH A COMPUTER?

Perhaps this question should have been asked first. A computer without some computing to be done is a rather woeful sight. Granted, the experimenter will undoubtedly learn a lot while assembling the parts of a microcomputer, and perhaps this in itself is sufficient justification for building the computer. Usually, however, the builder eventually plans to use the computer for some worthwhile purpose. Many times, the worthwhile purpose may develop only after the computer has been built and has been holding down a shelf in the workshop.

Your imagination is the limit. Program the computer to play games such as tic-tac-toe, blackjack, or poker. Maybe there is some application such as checkbook balancing or kitchen inventory control for which you could program it. For clubs or other groups, a microcomputer lends itself well to the management of membership lists and other record-keeping chores. As the heart of a home security system, a microcomputer could be programmed to react to different situations according to predetermined criteria.

Most important of all, remember that the microcomputer has evolved in a relatively short time, and will probably continue to evolve. As time goes by, the accepted ways of dealing with certain electronic circuits may become obsolete, and techniques yet to be discovered will become commonplace.

chapter 2

BASIC COMPUTER CONCEPTS

Perhaps the computers of tomorrow will operate in a way that we have yet to discover. Breakthroughs are being made nearly every day. In the meantime, if we examine the micro-computers of today, we see that, although they are in a different physical form from their full-sized counterparts, much the same design architecture has been employed in both types. This architecture is mainly due to the fact that digital computers operate by using the binary number system, which demands a certain type of logical approach to performing various types of computer operations. We see, therefore, a kind of mimicking of the full-sized computers by this new breed of machine. This leads us to believe that there are some basic concepts about computers in general that can be applied to the micro-computer as well. Of course, there are exceptions to, and variations on, these basic concepts, but generally the processing objectives are the same, and the user of the microcomputer can analyze the different types in order to choose the one best suited for the intended application.

As shown in Fig. 2-1, there are five main parts to a computer. These five parts are found, in one form or another, in every digital computer, whether it is the massive system used by an insurance company to keep track of its premiums, or a microcomputer that is used to control a model railroad. These five main ingredients are:

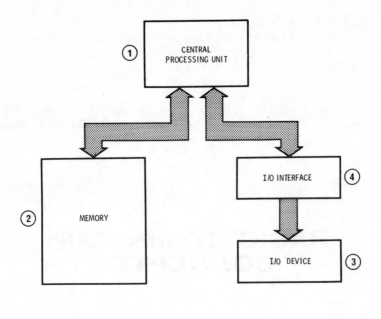

Fig. 2-1. The five main parts to a computer.

1. Central processing unit.
2. Memory.
3. Input/output devices.
4. Input/output interfaces.
5. Program.

1. *Central processing unit* (CPU).
   The "brain" of the computer—this is where the actual computing is done. The CPU usually controls all the operations of the computer.
2. *Memory.*
   An electronic storage medium used to hold the program which instructs the CPU and other components of the computer.

3. *Input/output devices.*
   These are the link between man and machine. They vary in type and complexity according to the processing requirements. Input/output devices include keyboards, teletypewriters, video displays, and so on.
4. *Input/output interfaces.*
   These are the "middlemen" between the CPU and the I/O device. They provide the actual hard-wired control of the I/O device, according to the commands that are issued by the CPU.
5. *Program.*
   Without the program, a computer is no more than a handful of parts that sits there and draws current. The program coordinates the operations of the computer in order to perform some desired process.

Each of these five main ingredients will be explored in more detail in this chapter. The emphasis will be on the logical operation of these elements within the computer. Chapter 3 will deal with these five elements from a "hardware" viewpoint, discussing the various electronic aspects of each.

CENTRAL PROCESSING UNIT (CPU)

Every computer has some sort of central processing unit (CPU), which is the "brain" of the computing machine. The CPU is a combination of several "parts," interconnected in such a way as to permit certain logical operations to be performed. Computers of ten years ago required a fairly large enclosure to house the components of their CPUs. Swing-out logic gates holding rows of pc boards, interconnected by garden-hose-sized cable, were not an uncommon sight. Today, the microcomputer uses a CPU that is contained in an LSI chip. This is the *microprocessor,* which, by itself, is not a computer but is the main component in any microcomputer.

Simple Binary Information—the Bit

Microprocessors are digital devices using digital logic concepts to accomplish some processing goal. This digital logic, or binary logic, as it is sometimes called, is based on the fact that certain electronic circuits can be either *on* or *off,* the state being determined by their operating characteristics. These provide a means of defining two "states" or "conditions."

If we have a single circuit, which is to be used to indicate one or the other of two possible conditions, this circuit is said to contain a *binary digit,* or *bit* of information. This bit can designate "on" or "off." Another frequent expression is that the bit is a "1" or a "0." This terminology corresponds to the only two numerals in the binary number system. The binary and other number systems are described in further detail in Appendix A.

When we have only one bit, it's plain to see that we can represent only one of two situations. As in Fig. 2-2, this would be sufficient to tell us whether we had left the front porchlight on or off, but for any serious computing, it simply will not do.

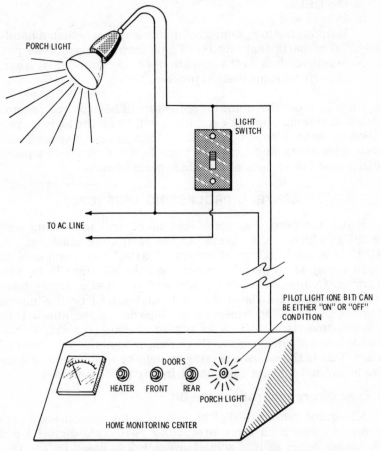

PORCH LIGHT

LIGHT SWITCH

TO AC LINE

PILOT LIGHT (ONE BIT) CAN BE EITHER "ON" OR "OFF" CONDITION

DOORS

HEATER FRONT REAR

PORCH LIGHT

HOME MONITORING CENTER

Fig. 2-2. Porchlight circuit yielding one bit of information.

Combining Bits to Make Words

To be able to represent more than two conditions with binary logic, several bits may be connected in such a way as to provide a more usable logical unit called the *word*. A word may have any number of bits, depending on several factors to be discussed later. Also, it is convenient if the number of bits in a word is some exact power of 2 (4, 8, 16, and so on). Each word can then be used to represent many different conditions, depending on how many bits are used to make up the word. For example, with 4 bits, we can represent 16 different conditions, by choosing various combinations of "bit patterns," or 1's and 0's. With 8 bits, we can represent 256 different conditions. Thus, we can see that the total number of different combinations of the bits in a word is 2^n, where n is the number of bits.

When a microprocessor manufacturer decides to use a certain "word length" (number of bits in a word), the requirements of the CPU are directly involved. If, for example, it is decided to use 8-bit words, then all of the information with which the CPU is to work will be in the form of 8-bit words. This implies that the CPU must be built to process 8-bit words, and that some other word length, say 4 bits, would be meaningless. There are processors that are built to handle variable-length words, but this requires a significant amount of consideration on the part of the programmer, in order to keep everything straight. For the most part, microprocessors of today are fixed word length machines. The most common word length is 8 bits. There are some 16-bit machines, and these are considerably more powerful, since approximately 65,000 different conditions can be represented with 16 bits, as compared to only 256 combinations for an 8-bit word length. Other microprocessors use 4-bit words. These are not as powerful as higher-bit computers in the sense that they cannot represent as many different conditions. However, they are adequate for many of the simple applications that do not require as much complexity.

Using Words to Define Instructions

Perhaps the one single attribute that differentiates the microprocessor from other machines is that it can be "told" what to do. This is accomplished by using words which contain a bit pattern that is meaningful to the processor. This meaningfulness is determined by the manufacturer. One bit pattern may be used to tell the processor to add two numbers. Another bit pattern may be used to tell it to print a character on a teletypewriter. Another bit pattern may have no meaning to the processor at all.

The group of bit patterns that the manufacturer decides will have some meaning is called the *instruction set*. These instructions will tell the processor what operation it is to perform and, in many cases, how the operation is to be modified due to the bit pattern contained in some other word. The variety of different operations defined by the instruction set is determined by the manufacturer, in order to fulfill some design criteria. Most instruction sets include some standard arithmetic operations, e.g., addition and subtraction. Also, some "bit manipulation" instructions are usually provided, as well as the frequently used logical operations AND, OR, and EOR (or XOR). Other than these, different instruction sets contain various sorts of operations depending upon the intended application of the processor. Some will be prolific in input/output instructions, if the application demands complicated input or output procedures. Others offer more sophisticated arithmetic instructions in order to process mathematically oriented problems with greater precision.

As shown in Fig. 2-3, the processor cannot distinguish between bit patterns that are instructions and those that are not instructions. If the processor should accidentally try to execute "data" instead of an instruction, usually an error is created. Some processors contain circuitry that can tell if an invalid instruction is being executed, and will halt the process.

Most processing objectives will require that a certain sequence of steps be performed. For example, suppose that we want to compute the area of a circle using the simple formula

$$\text{area} = \pi \times (\text{radius})^2$$

Since we know that the value of π is a constant, we can rewrite the equation as follows:

$$\text{area} = (3.14) \times (\text{radius})^2$$

Now, suppose that we can somehow "input" the radius of the circle into the computer, and that the computer, after calculating the area, will "output" the answer. The sequence of operations involved here would be:

1. INPUT the radius.
2. SQUARE the radius.
3. MULTIPLY the radius by the value of π.
4. OUTPUT the answer.

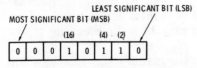

(A) Binary representation of the number 22, in an 8-bit word.

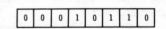

(B) The bit pattern representing an instruction to add two numbers.

Fig. 2-3. Bit patterns for a data element and for an instruction.

We can appreciate that we would not obtain the correct answer if the operations were not executed in this sequence. For example, if we were to reverse the order of steps 2 and 3, we would be multiplying the radius by the value of π before we squared it, which would yield a totally different answer.

The Instruction Register

Only one instruction can be executed by the processor at any given time. The result of executing one instruction may set up

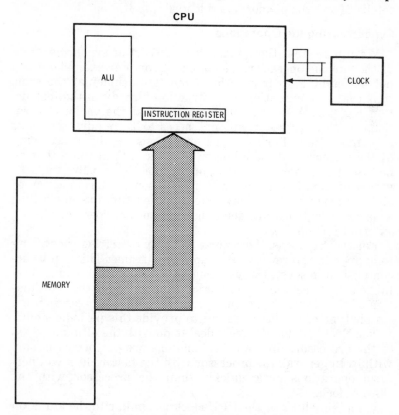

Fig. 2-4. Simplified CPU configuration.

certain conditions that are required for the execution of the next instruction. The sequence of instructions that is to be performed by the processor is usually stored in memory of some kind, which will be discussed in further detail later in this chapter. As each instruction is needed, it is fetched from the memory and put into the instruction register (Fig. 2-4), which is a circuit that can electronically hold one word.

Electronic circuits in the processor "decode" the word in the instruction register and, based on the bit pattern of that word, determine what operation is to be performed. The 1 and 0 bits in the word contained by the instruction register can be thought of as "connections," each one being used to shape the circuitry in the processor to enable it to execute the desired operation. The instruction register will contain the instruction all during the time that it is being executed. When it is finished with one instruction, the next instruction in the sequence is fetched from the memory, and loaded into it.

Synchronizing the Operations

We can see that there must be some sort of synchronization of the various operations of the processor. For example, it can not be fetching an instruction from the memory at the same time that it is executing an instruction already in the instruction register. Also, we must consider that the various operations of the processor will not necessarily require the same amount of time. For example, operations requiring accessing of the memory will take longer to execute than those that do not use the memory. Likewise, operations that involve the activating of some I/O device will initiate some external action of another machine. This may take a million times as much time as is required to execute some instruction that does not use any external I/O device.

For these reasons, there must be a way of getting everything to happen in reference to the same time frame. This can be accomplished in several ways. Some processors use a quartz crystal "clock" to establish a universal time pulse for the coordination of the events that occur internally. Other processors use a simple type of oscillator circuit to provide this periodic signal.

The clock will have a great deal to do with the ultimate speed of the processor, since all the functions are performed in step with it. In general, the processor with the faster clock will perform operations more quickly than the processor with the slower clock.

We might think of the CPU clock as similar to the crank on the old organ grinder. The faster the crank is turned, the faster the mechanism inside produces the music.

Arithmetic/Logic Unit (ALU)

The arithmetic/logic unit (ALU) is the part of the CPU used to perform the arithmetic and logical operations that are defined by the instruction set. The ALU contains electronic circuits that perform binary arithmetic as described in Appendix A of this book.

There are various binary arithmetic operations that the ALU circuits can perform. The circuits are directly controlled by a part of the CPU that decodes the instruction in the instruction register and sets up the ALU for the desired function. Most binary arithmetic is based on the "addition" algorithm, or procedure. Subtraction is carried out as a kind of "negative addition." Multiplication and division are generally not performed as discrete instructions, but rather as chains of additions or subtractions under program control. ALUs found in the more powerful microprocessors do offer multiplication and division, as well as other arithmetic operations, in the form of "hardware" circuits which are accessible through one machine instruction.

Arithmetic Modes

There are several types of arithmetic modes used in the microprocessors of today. The most commonly encountered are *signed binary* and *unsigned binary*.

Signed binary arithmetic uses the "leftmost," or most significant, bit (MSB) of the word to indicate the sign (positive or negative) of the number that is represented by the remainder of the bits in the word. The usual convention here is that, in a negative number, the sign bit will be *set* (equal to 1), and in a positive number, the sign bit will be *cleared* (equal to 0). Generally, negative numbers are stored in a "complemented" form which, as described in Appendix A, makes the binary subtraction operation a negative addition. It is important to note that using one of the bits in each word to indicate the sign of a number stored in the word reduces the range (or absolute value) of the number that can be stored in the remaining bits of the word. Thus, in an 8-bit word, using signed binary arithmetic, we can represent numbers from -128 to $+127$, and of course zero. This is still 256 total different combinations, but even when unsigned numbers are represented, their maximum size is also limited. As we will see in Chapter 4 on programming, this word size limitation can cause the programmer some serious problems in the generation of memory location addresses.

The unsigned binary arithmetic mode, as its name implies, does not offer the ability to represent positive and negative numbers. The MSB of each word is *not* used to indicate the sign of the number that is stored in the word. Therefore, the entire word can be used to store the number. This allows us to store a larger number in each word, but we must be sure that this number will never have to be negative, in order for the operations using it to have some meaning.

The ALU in most microprocessors is capable of handling both these kinds of arithmetic, and of distinguishing between them. Different instructions are used by the CPU to direct the ALU to perform the desired mode of arithmetic. Some microprocessors have ALUs that are capable of doing arithmetic operations on much larger numbers, which may be stored by using more than one word. This ability is another indicator of the amount of processing power that any given microprocessor

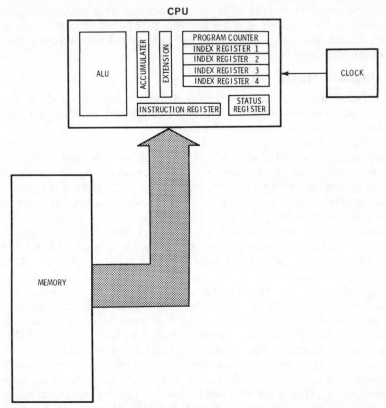

Fig. 2-5. CPU registers.

may have. For some applications, the simple combination of signed and unsigned arithmetic is more than adequate, and therefore the user must evaluate his processing needs to determine what criteria to use when selecting a microprocessor.

Accumulator and Other Internal Registers

Generally, a number of hardware registers are contained within the CPU. These are used for several purposes by the

CPU itself or by the ALU. All microprocessors contain some combination of registers.

The register most commonly associated with the microprocessor is called the *accumulator* (see Fig. 2-5). This register is the primary register used during many of the operations that are defined by the instruction set. It is used by the ALU to hold one element of data during an arithmetic operation. It is also directly accessible to the CPU as a working area for many non-arithmetic operations. The accumulator generally has the same number of bits as the defined word length of the particular microprocessor. It is used many times during the execution of a program as the threshold to the memory. The instruction set usually includes some kind of "load" operation, during which the contents of some memory location are loaded into the accumulator. Also, the instruction sets usually include a "store" operation, which causes the contents of the accumulator to be stored at some prescribed memory location.

Probably the next most common internal register found in microprocessors is the *program counter* (PC). This is used to hold the memory location address of the word of memory with which the CPU is concerned at any given time. As we will see in Chapter 4, a "program" is a sequence of instructions that are stored in the memory in the order that they are to be executed. Each time that an instruction has completed execution, the next instruction must be fetched from the memory. The program counter is used by the CPU to keep track of where in the program the current operation is located. Each time that a new instruction is fetched from the memory, the program counter is modified to contain the memory address of that instruction. The program counter is usually accessible by the program, which means that as a result of processing certain instructions, the PC itself may be changed, thereby forcing the program execution to be taken up at some other point.

The CPU usually has one or more *index registers* available for the storage of information that is going to be used by the program many times. Index registers are also used to hold addresses of areas of the memory that are to be "stepped through," such as tables of numbers. Chapter 4, on programming, shows several examples of how index registers are used by the program. Other uses are hardware type features that the manufacturer has built into the CPU, such as special "interrupt vectors," and these features will be described in more detail in the discussion of I/O interfaces.

In general, the number and size of the hardware registers is another parameter in determining the computing power of a given microprocessor—the more registers, the better, in most cases. As we shall learn in the chapter on programming, these registers can get used up quickly, leaving the programmer with no option but to use a word of memory for a job that really should be done by a register.

Another register generally found in a CPU is the *extension register*. The extension register is normally used in conjunction with the accumulator for performing "double-precision" arithmetic. This is an arithmetic mode in which each number is represented by two words of memory, both of which must be involved in any operation by the ALU. The extension register is normally used to hold the least significant bits (LSBs) of the number, while the accumulator is used to hold the most significant bits (MSBs) of the number. In this way, the two registers are connected together to form one large arithmetic register. The extension register is also used for other purposes depending upon the manufacturer's objectives in designing the microprocessor. One microprocessor uses this register as a "serial I/O port," where the input data are fed into the extension register's MSB, and the output data are fed out of the LSB of the register.

Another hardware register common to all computers is the *status register*. This is usually a one-word register that is used to keep track of various conditions within the computer. Each bit in the status register word may be assigned a certain meaning by the manufacturer. For example, a certain bit may be "set" if an arithmetic carry occurs as a result of performing some operation in the ALU. A carry occurs when the result of the arithmetic is too large to be represented by the particular word length of the CPU. Another example of the use of this register might be a bit that is used to indicate whether or not some I/O device is requesting service. Perhaps a bit is used by the I/O device to tell the CPU that it has finished the last operation that it was commanded to perform, and is ready to perform the next operation.

Here is another way to determine just how much computing power a particular microprocessor can offer. The complexity of the status register will give the user a pretty good idea of the "smartness" of the microprocessor.

A *storage address register* is found in various microprocessors. This register is used in conjunction with memory accessing. The storage address register is used to hold the memory address of the data that are being either "loaded" from memory or "stored" into memory.

Microprocessors may or may not have a *storage buffer register*. This is simply a hardware device that holds an image of the contents of the memory location addressed in the storage address register. In some microprocessors, all data that are transferred to and from the memory are routed through this register. This pertains to instructions as well as data, the instructions being routed to the CPU decoding logic, and the data being normally bound for the accumulator or one of the other registers.

Communicating With the CPU

In the previous paragraphs, we have learned about the insides of a typical CPU. We know that CPUs can do various types of arithmetic, that they can interpret certain bit patterns as instructions, and that they have several hardware registers that are used in various ways to aid in the processing. However, the CPU must be given all the information that is pertinent to the operation that is desired. We must furnish the CPU with the instruction and also tell it where to get the data to be operated upon and where to put the result after the operation has been completed. For this purpose, there are communication lines into, and out of, the CPU. These lines are usually a parallel to the binary format that the CPU uses for all of its operations. Therefore, if the word length is eight bits, there will be eight lines connected to the CPU in order to transmit data in or out. This group of lines is called a *bus*, and there are three different types of busses leading into, and out of, the CPU (Fig. 2-6):

1. Data bus.
2. Address bus.
3. Control bus.

We will examine each of these busses individually.

Data Bus—The data bus is used for the transmission of data in or out of the CPU. There are as many lines in this bus as there are bits in the data words for the particular microprocessor. The most common use of the data bus is in transferring information from memory into the CPU, and from the CPU into the memory.

There are some CPUs that have a separate data bus for *reading*, or transferring data from memory to the CPU, and for *writing*, or transferring data from the CPU into the memory. For the most part, this architecture has been avoided since it requires twice as many lines as the read/write combination bus method. In the latter method, the same bus is used for both reading and writing data.

Address Bus—This group of lines is used to select the individual location to or from which the transfer of data is to be made. The most common usage of the address bus is in conjunction with the memory. This bus will carry the address of the location in memory that is being accessed by the CPU at any given time.

Some manufacturers have combined the data and address busses into one, shared bus. This is accomplished by multiplexing data and addresses on the same lines. As we might imagine, this requires some sort of synchronization so that, at any time, the CPU can tell whether the bus is carrying data or addresses.

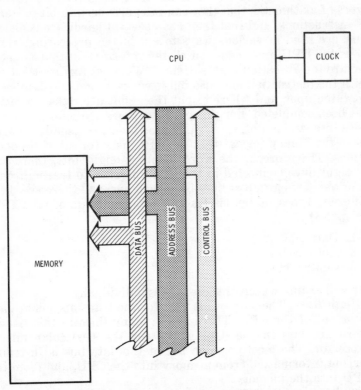

Fig. 2-6. Communicating with the CPU.

It is also possible to address I/O devices as though they were memory locations. This is done by several microprocessors currently on the market. As long as the I/O device does not interfere with the other uses of the bus, the CPU won't be able to tell the difference.

As we will see in the next section of this chapter, there are many addresses of memory, and perhaps many addresses of I/O devices that need to be represented on the address bus.

Therefore, in most processors, we will find that the address bus is wider (greater number of bits) than the word length of the machine.

Control Bus—The control bus is not quite the same kind of group of lines as are the data bus and the address bus. Rather, it is a group of several "dedicated" lines that are each used for some special purpose. Most processors have some sort of a control bus, some more complex and offering more control than others. One of the things that the control bus is used for is to *reset* the processor. This reset function clears the registers in the CPU to all 0's and prepares the processor for the beginning of some program. The reset is normally accomplished by some sort of a front-panel control which is connected to the reset line on the control bus. Likewise, once the processor is operating and actually executing instructions, we would probably desire to have some means to stop everything. Most processors have a separate line that, when switched, causes the processor to stop after completion of the instruction currently being executed.

There are a multitude of other control functions that various manufacturers employ in the design of their processors. Some are used when more than one CPU is to be using the same memory or I/O devices. Others are used to change the CPU operations during execution.

Here is another area for comparing the various microprocessors that are available. How many user control functions are provided for on the control bus?

There is one "bus" that we have not discussed. This is the *internal bus* inside the CPU chip which is used to connect all of the various registers and to connect the ALU with the instruction decoding logic. This is not a concept that is peculiar to the microprocessor. However, since it is contained within the chip itself, it is not really available to the user's program. We will take a closer look at this bus in the next chapter as we compare some of the microprocessors' hardware features.

MEMORY

As we have seen in the previous paragraphs, the CPU executes a sequence of instructions, which we call a program, in order to fulfill some processing goal. Since the CPU can deal with only one instruction at any given time, there must be a place to store all of the instructions of the program, and to fetch them, one at a time, for execution. This is the primary use of memory by the computer—to store the program instructions. The memory may also hold data (for example, a constant such as the value of π). In some cases, large tables of data are stored in the memory in order that they may be used as a reference by some program during execution. Whether used for instructions or data, the memory is utilized in the same way for both.

Types of Memory

Although the basic reasons for memory, and the ways that memory is utilized, are the same for both instructions and data, there are several different types of memory, each offering a special feature for the user. We will discuss five of these most common types:

1. *Core*—magnetic core memory.
2. *RAM*—random-access monolithic memory.
3. *ROM*—read-only memory.
4. *PROM*—programmable ROM.
5. *EPROM*—erasable programmable ROM.

Core Memory—Magnetic core memory has been the most popular form of computer memory for quite a few years. This type of memory is known as *nonvolatile* because it will retain the information that is stored in it for an indefinite length of time, and it need not have power applied or be refreshed. Over the years, this form of memory has become reasonably priced. However, the drawbacks of its use with a microprocessor are twofold. First of all, magnetic core does require quite a bit of power in order to write into it. Secondly, its physical size is just not compatible with the LSI technology of microprocessor chips. So, it looks as though the use of magnetic core memory may be waning. At least in the microprocessor fields, the alternatives are much more desirable.

RAM Memory—This memory actually should be called "monolithic random-access memory," but since it has become the most popular type of memory associated with the microprocessor, its name has been shortened simply to RAM. The term *random access* means that any word in the memory may be accessed, without having to go through all the other words to get to it. This memory, being monolithic (that is, being contained in an integrated-circuit chip), is much more suitable to the microprocessor. The power requirement for these memory chips is very similar to that of the microprocessor itself. The signal level necessary to write into this memory is relatively small. The only drawback of RAM memory is that it is a *volatile* form of memory. This means that when the power is removed from the chip, all the memory content is lost. When the power is returned, the content of memory will be unknown. On the other hand, the power consumption of these memory chips is so small that it is feasible to leave them "powered up" all the time. The only eventuality to contend with then would be the occasional power failure or brownout that might cause the loss of the content of memory.

ROM Memory—Read-only memory is very similar to RAM except for one thing. It is not possible to write into ROM memory the way it is to write into RAM. This type of memory is useful, then, only as a source of information, and it cannot be used by the program to store any data or instructions. When purchasing a ROM, the user must specify to the manufacturer exactly what the user wants to be in the memory. The manufacturer, using special equipment, prepares the ROM with the information that the user requests. This information may then be read as many times as desired, and ROM does not require that the power be supplied continuously in order that the information be retained. So ROM memory is also nonvolatile, as is core memory. The ROM memory is useful for such things as the storing of a table of information that is only referred to and never changed. Also, some programs that are required frequently can be stored in ROM and then read into a RAM memory to be executed. Some programs can be executed directly from the ROM, since each instruction is fetched from the memory, and passed on to the CPU instruction decoding logic. If, however, there are any parts of the program that are altered during execution, they cannot be left in the ROM, and they must be read into the RAM memory in order to be executed properly.

PROM Memory—PROM, or programmable ROM, is very much like simple ROM memory, except that it can be programmed by the user in the field. The PROM chips can be purchased blank and then be programmed by using a special machine. Once programmed, this memory behaves the same as the ROM. That is, it can be read as many times as desired but cannot be written into. Also, it is not necessary to supply power continuously to PROM memory in order to preserve the information. In other words, it is nonvolatile memory.

EPROM Memory—This is one of the latest types of monolithic memory. It is called erasable programmable ROM. It can be programmed in the field by the user, and it can also be erased and reprogrammed with different information. Once it has been programmed, the EPROM memory acts just the same as ROM. Again, this is a memory that cannot be written into, but it can be read as many times as necessary.

One way of combining memory types is shown in the block diagram of Fig. 2-7.

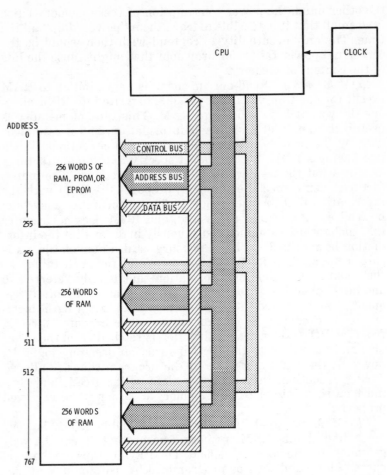

Fig. 2-7. Combining RAM and ROM memories.

Organization and Addressing of Memory

In organizing and addressing memory, the first fact that we should remember is that memory for a digital computer will have to be in binary form, because all information in a digital computer is stored in binary. Second, we must remember that each microprocessor has a word length that is determined by the manufacturer. This word length is the number of binary "bits" that are grouped together into one logical unit of information in binary. From these two facts, we can see that memory must be able to store information in binary words of the same length as the microprocessor word.

All the types of memory that were described in the last section are constructed so that they fulfill the requirements of binary memory. They are subdivided into words, each of which contains a bit pattern representing an instruction in the program or perhaps data which is to be operated upon by the computer program.

The next question is: How much memory is needed by the computer? This is a totally variable number which is dependent on several conditions. The complexity of the application for which the computer is going to be used is the first criterion for determining how much memory is needed. If there is going to be a need to store large amounts of data in memory, then the requirements may be determined by this fact. Certainly a program that would compute the area of circles would not require as much memory as a program to play chess, since program size is mainly a function of the number of instructions that are contained in the program.

Monolithic memory comes in very convenient IC packages, and, generally speaking, each chip contains some fixed number of words of memory. These chips may be grouped together to form however much memory is required.

Consider the addressing of memory. This is the ability to select any one of the many words of memory that we are likely to have available. When using the memory, the CPU must know where in the memory to find the next instruction, or possibly where to find some data that are to be used in the execution of an instruction. Therefore, the memory (already arranged in groups of bits to form words) is given numbered addresses for each word, much the same as all the people living on the same street have different addresses. This system of addressing makes it possible to store information at a specific memory address, and then later come back to exactly the right place to find it.

A number is assigned each word in memory, starting with 0 and continuing as high as need be for the amount of memory that is available. Then, any time that a particular word of information is to be referred to, its address may be used. The CPU can keep track of where it is in the program during execution, by storing the address of the location in the program counter. Each time that an instruction has completed execution, the program counter is incremented to contain the address of the next word in the memory, in which the next program instruction will be stored. (See Fig. 2-8.) In most cases, the program is stored in ascending sequence in the memory; that is, the beginning of the program is at a lower memory address than the end of the program.

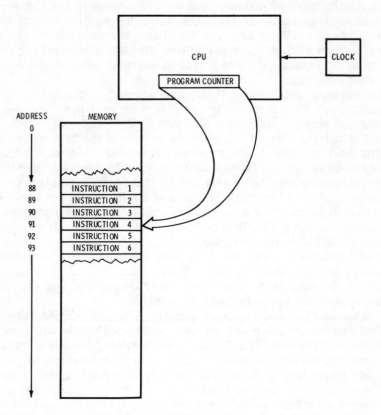

Fig. 2-8. Program counter "points" to the instruction being executed.

Reading From Memory

Reading from memory is the act of getting the information that is stored in the memory out of the memory and into some other place where it can be used. This is why earlier in this chapter we referred to this process as "loading" the contents of a memory location into a register. The contents of the memory location are not changed by the operation of reading from that memory location.

Writing Into Memory

Writing into memory is the process of putting some information into the memory for storage. Earlier in this chapter, we referred to this process as "storing" the contents of a register into a memory location. Of course, the writing process destroys the previous contents of the memory location and replaces them with the new information. This writing cannot be done with any kind of ROM memory, since there are no circuits in the ROM chip to receive the information.

INPUT/OUTPUT DEVICES

In this chapter about basic computer concepts, we started at the center with the CPU and worked our way to the "outside world." For it is in the outside world that the ultimate effect of the processing inside the computer will be felt. The computer's function will have significance for whoever will use this powerful instrument. Since humans are not equipped with address and data busses that can be connected directly to the computer, we must have some other way of communicating with it.

Many forms of information may be entered into the computer. Depending upon the application and the volume of information that is likely to be involved, there are several machines that can be connected to a computer. These machines are constructed so that they can be operated by humans. The machine translates the operations into signals that can be interpreted by the computer. Some of these devices translate the signals generated by the computer into a "human language." These machines are called *input/output devices*, or more simply, *I/O devices*.

It is not always necessary that the computer be connected to some "human" interface. In many applications, the computer is used as a controller of other machines. Some applications involve several computers communicating with each other. In all cases, however, some kind of an interface with the world is necessary. It may be as simple as two wires used to turn something on and off, or it may be as complex as several dozen video monitors giving flight information to passengers at the airport.

Simple Devices

Many computer applications, especially those suitable for microcomputer use, may not require the complex I/O devices found in the big commercial data processing installations. The processing objective may be as simple as that of a typical four-function calculator. In this case, we can see that there probably won't be a need for a high-speed printer. Going a step further in simplicity, sometimes it is desirable to be able to see what is going on in the computer at any given moment. Likewise, it is desirable to be able to change something in the computer at will. These are operations that a programmer would be concerned with if he had just executed his new program for the first time, and found that it wasn't working right.

Front-Panel Switches and Lights—These are the simplest form of I/O devices. (See Fig. 2-9.) They provide the user with the "switches and lights" necessary to determine what is going on inside the computer, and to change it if so desired. Fundamental to this form of I/O device is the fact that the user must deal with the computer in its own language—binary. This seems awkward at first, but after a little practice it becomes more natural. This device usually has one or more rows of toggle switches, each switch representing a bit in some register. Each row of switches then represents the bit pattern in the register. Corresponding to the switches is usually one or more rows of lights. (For obvious reasons, LEDs are more popularly used here than incandescent bulbs.) Each light also represents a bit in some register, and the row of lights represents the bit pattern in some register.

A typical use of this type of I/O device might be as follows. Suppose you are the programmer, and your new program isn't working. You think you might know what's wrong, but in order to verify your suspicions, you need to find out what bit pattern is stored at some particular memory address. You must enter the memory address of the location as a binary number. You do this by setting the bit pattern that represents that number into the switches. You turn the switches on that correspond to 1 bits, and turn off the switches that correspond to 0 bits. Then you press the button that is labeled LOAD ADDRESS REGISTER. This loads the address register with the memory address that is represented by the switches. Next, you press the button labeled EXAMINE. This causes the contents of the memory location that was selected to be displayed as a binary bit pattern in the row of lights. An "on" light corresponds to a 1 bit; an "off" light corresponds to a 0 bit. Now you can interpret the binary bit pattern and determine if your guess was right or if you must look further for the answer to the problem.

The drawbacks to this type of I/O device are self-evident. The operator must resort to using the computer's binary language in order to do what is desired. The chance of making an error while doing this is great, even for one who is quite familiar with binary. Entering one bit in the wrong position in the word will cause an error. However, if this type of operation is required only once in a while, the user can take his time, and make sure that everything is done correctly.

Hex Keyboard and Seven-Segment Display—Here is a slightly more sophisticated I/O device. It lightens the load on the user as far as having to think in binary. With this type of I/O device, the same kinds of operations can be accomplished as with the switches and lights. The main difference here is

(A) Switch array.

(B) Front panel.

Courtesy National Semiconductor Corp.

Fig. 2-9. Front-panel switches and lights.

that this device makes the computer do some of the work. It converts the information back and forth between binary and another form of notation called *hexadecimal*.

The hexadecimal number system is described in more detail in Appendix A, but, briefly, it is a kind of abbreviated binary format. "Hex" is a base-16 number system, which means that 16 different numerals are used. This is certainly convenient, as sixteen is an integral power of 2 ($16 = 2^4$). This means that a group of four bits in a word can be grouped together and represented by one hex digit.

The hex keyboard looks much like a regular calculator-type keyboard, except that we see that there are a few more keys (Fig. 2-10). Now, instead of having to set the position of each of several switches to enter a bit pattern, the user need only press the key that represents each four-bit group in the bit pattern.

The seven-segment display takes the place of the row of lights that represented the bit pattern being "examined." Here again, the binary information to be displayed is converted to the hexadecimal form and is then used to turn on the correct combination of the "segments" in order to produce the visual display.

We can see that this form of I/O device would make debugging a program much easier to achieve than in the previous example. This flexibility does not come free. In order to make this type of I/O device function, significantly more electronics is needed than was necessary with the switch and light approach. Many such I/O devices require special programs inside the computer to make them work. In any case, the difference in complexity between the switches and lights and the hex keyboard and seven-segment display is quite noticeable.

Moderately Complex Devices

Beyond the two examples of simple I/O devices given in the last section is a whole variety of devices used for every conceivable means of communicating with the computer. We will take a brief look at three of the most popular types of I/O devices that offer the user a lot of flexibility in various applications.

ASCII Keyboard—First of all, the word *ASCII* is an acronym for *A*merican *S*tandard *C*ode for *I*nformation *I*nterchange. ASCII is pronounced "ass-key." ASCII is a binary code that is used to represent other forms of information. For example, the characters of the alphabet can be represented in ASCII, each as a distinct bit pattern. Likewise, the numerals of the regular decimal number system (0–9) as well as various

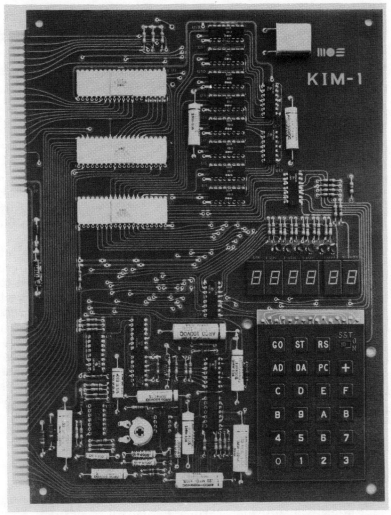

Courtesy MOS Technology, Inc.

Fig. 2-10. Hex keyboard and seven-segment display.

special characters such as periods, commas, hyphens, and so on, can all be represented using this code.

An ASCII keyboard looks very much like a regular typewriter keyboard (Fig. 2-11). It has keys for each of the characters in the alphabet, as well as for the special characters, laid out in the familiar pattern for operation by both hands. Each key is simply a switch that, when pressed, causes the special electronic circuits connected to it to produce the ASCII bit pattern for that character. This bit pattern, then, can be sent along to the computer with ease since it is in a form that the computer recognizes.

The ASCII keyboard is an "input" device only. There is no way that it can be hooked up in reverse to serve as an "output" device. As an input device, it is considered quite flexible, since the human operator can easily operate the keys, and the computer can easily accept the ASCII coded character that it produces. There are other considerations, however, since the electronic circuits that are used in conjunction with the keyboard are themselves quite complex. One most obvious problem arises when the operator presses more than one key at a time. So, although this device offers ease of operation, it also requires "babysitting" hardware in order for it to be utilized fully.

Fig. 2-11. ASCII keyboard.

Teletype—The Teletype has long been a favorite I/O device for small computers and large ones too. Its main attributes are that it has a typewriterlike keyboard and it also has a printing unit which can provide "hard copy" output if desired. (See Fig. 2-12.) Although we usually find that the keyboard and the printer are physically in the same cabinet, it is important to note that they are two distinctly separate devices, and are not mechanically interconnected as in a regular typewriter. They may be connected, if so desired, so that when a key is pressed on the keyboard, the corresponding character will be printed by the printer.

The Teletype is more of a mechanical device than the ASCII keyboard, which is mainly an electronic device with the only mechanics being in the key switches. Pressing a key on the Teletype keyboard causes the mechanics inside to set up a series of switch contacts, making a binary representation of the character selected. In some machines, this binary representation is in the same ASCII code that the previous keyboard device produced. In other machines, the particular code

Fig. 2-12. Teletype console with paper tape.

that is used may be different. Any code can be used, as long as the computer that is to receive the coded information is programmed to recognize it.

The Teletype printer, used as an output device, operates in a similar mechanical fashion. The characters to be printed are sent to the printer in whatever binary code the printer is designed to operate with. As each bit pattern is sent to the printer, it is used to set up a series of selector solenoids which cause the desired type bar to strike the paper.

We can see why this particular I/O device is so popular, since it is both an input device and an output device in one unit. It also requires some external electronic circuits in order to be able to "talk" to the computer, but the usefulness of the system is increased considerably in most cases.

Paper Tape—Paper tape itself is not an I/O device. Rather, it is a storage medium making use of tape made out of paper. The tape is about one inch (2.54 centimeters) in width and of normal paper thickness, and comes in large rolls of several hundred feet (meters). Holes can be punched into this tape to form bit patterns of binary coded information. This information may be coded in ASCII or some other code, depending on the user's application.

A *paper-tape reader* is a machine used to detect the holes that are punched into the tape, and to create an electronic bit pattern to be sent to the computer. These machines can run at a fairly fast speed, depending on the model, and they make it possible for the user to reload the same information many times into the computer with very little effort. Tapes containing programs that are used often can be punched and stored in a small area and then read into the computer when they are to be executed.

There is also a machine called a *paper-tape punch*. This machine does as its name implies. Information, represented as an electronic bit pattern, is sent to the paper-tape punch from the computer. The bit pattern is used to set up the correct combination of punch dies so that the holes will be punched into the tape in the same pattern. As each bit pattern (or word) is punched into the tape, the machine pulls the tape through the punch dies so that they form a continuous series of words of information encoded in the holes in paper tape.

Many Teletype machines have paper-tape equipment attached to them. This is a very convenient arrangement. In such cases, the user has four I/O devices in one unit: a keyboard, a printer, a paper-tape reader, and a paper-tape punch. This makes a very simple yet flexible computer system.

Complex Devices

Any means of speeding up the rate at which information is transferred between the computer and the "real world" will result in the greater usefulness of the computer. Obviously, the more complex the information to be transferred, the more complex the I/O device must be. In this section, we will take a look at some of these complex devices. Only a few are represented here, since there are so many devices created for special applications.

Modems—The word *modem* is a contraction of two words: "*mo*dulator," which is a device that encodes information into some form of transmittable code, and "*dem*odulator," which is a device that decodes incoming information. Thus, a modem is a device used in conjunction with the sending and receiving of information, to and from a computer.

The main purpose of a modem is to access a computer from a remote location, via the telephone lines. It converts the information to be transmitted into a series of audio tones. These tones are sent over the telephone line and must be "demodulated" at the receiving end by another modem. In some cases, these modems are simply "black boxes" that perform their function with little or no attention from the user. Other applications enhance the modem, perhaps adding some memory in order to store a simple program which will direct the operation of the modem or to provide an area to "buffer" the transmission of the information. Some modems even have a microprocessor inside them and could almost be called a computer.

Magnetic Tape—Magnetic tape is similar in many respects to paper tape, which was previously discussed. It, too, is a storage medium, and consists of the same kind of magnetic tape as that used for the recording of audio signals by a tape recorder. There are several different sizes of tape which are used for this purpose. The most common magnetic tape format (Fig. 2-13) in use with microcomputers is the familiar cassette cartridge.

The basic idea here is the same as that in the recording of music, except that instead of music we are recording binary information (1's and 0's) in a magnetic format that can later be read to re-create the binary information and feed it back into the computer. Although the cassette storage devices are quite a bit more sophisticated than the regular garden-variety cassette recorders, the latter can be converted for use in a microcomputer system.

An important thing to remember about magnetic tape is that, due to the fact that the tape is wound onto reels, the information is available only in a sequential manner. That is, if the desired information is somewhere near the end of the tape, the machine must read through all the information that precedes it on the tape, until the sought-after information is found. There is no way that the machine can go directly to the information.

Magnetic Disk—Magnetic disk is also a form of "secondary memory" used by the computer to store information which would take up too much room to store in RAM feasibly. The disk can be likened to a phonograph record, except that there are no grooves. Instead, the information is recorded magnetically, just as it is on magnetic tape.

The major difference between disk and tape storage is that the "head," which is used to read or write the information onto the magnetic disk, can be positioned so that any information is accessible, regardless of where it may be stored physically on the surface of the disk, without having to go through all the

Fig. 2-13. Magnetic tape I/O device.

other information to get to it. This gives the magnetic disk device much greater speed and flexibility than the magnetic tape device.

Video Display Modules (*VDMs*)—A video display module is an output device that uses a televisionlike screen to display information to the user. (See Fig. 2-14.) This information may be in the form of the characters of the alphabet and other symbols meaningful to the user. It may also be presented as a picture, graph, map, or whatever the particular application may dictate.

This device is quite a complex one. We can well imagine that the process necessary to display a screen full of printed information involves some sophisticated electronics. Some video display units incorporate large amounts of their own memory to store the information to be displayed on the screen. Others

Fig. 2-14. Video display module with keyboard.

even have a microprocessor inside them to manage the display operation.

Optical Scanners—An optical scanner is a device that can "see" certain things. It works mainly on the ability of various photoelectric components to distinguish between light and dark.

Optical scanners are very special-purpose input devices which are being used by industry for all kinds of functions, including measurement taking, recognition of various symbols, and, most recently, the Universal Product Coding system that we see printed on almost everything we buy at the store today. In this system, each product is marked with a bar code consisting of several dark lines of various widths, printed on a light background (Fig. 2-15). The scanner detects these lines and sends the product code along to the computer in binary. The computer then uses the code as a key to locate the information stored in memory regarding the particular product. The computer uses this information to operate the cash register, adding the value of the goods just scanned to the total for the given customer.

INPUT/OUTPUT INTERFACES

In the previous section, we have discussed various kinds of I/O devices, from the simple front-panel switches and lights

Fig. 2-15. UPC symbol.

to the complex optical scanner. We have seen that these are the interface between man and machine. These I/O devices, however, cannot simply be "plugged in" to the computer and be expected to work. There is a significant amount of interfacing that must be done between machine and machine. Fig. 2-16 shows one kind of interface.

Control Lines

One of the most essential parts of I/O interfacing is that of controlling the device. For example, if we are using a magnetic-

Fig. 2-16. I/O interface for cassette tape.

tape storage device with the computer, we will want to be able to start and stop the tape transport mechanism at will, usually under control of the program. In general, control lines are used to operate a mechanical device, at the will of the program.

Status Lines

Closely associated with the control lines, these lines are used so that the computer can determine the condition of an I/O device. This is necessary, for example, if the program is ready to issue a command to the Teletype to print a character, and the machine is still in the process of printing the previous character. A status line will tell the computer that the printer is busy and is not ready to receive the next character yet. When the printing operation is completed, the status line will indicate to the computer that the printer is ready to perform the next operation.

Another example of the use of a status line is in the operation of the ASCII keyboard. When a key is depressed, a status line will indicate to the computer that someone has pressed the key and that there is information ready to be entered. Sometimes another line is used to tell the computer that more than one key is being pressed at the moment, and to ignore the data.

Data Lines and Buffers

Of course, there must be some means of actually getting the information into, or out of, the computer. This is the purpose of the data lines. In most cases, the processor's data bus is used for this purpose (Fig. 2-17). Some processors treat I/O functions as though they were simply references to memory.

Usually the computer has a limited ability to send and receive information on the data lines. In this case, the I/O interface must also contain circuitry that can buffer or temporarily store the information sent from the computer so that it can be modified in some way to make it usable by the device. In the case of the video display module, the buffer may be large enough to hold several "lines" of information to be displayed.

Synchronizing and Timing

When some types of I/O devices are used, the transfer of information between the computer and the device must take place under very close timing specifications. This is especially true for devices that communicate with the computer by using only two wires. These are called *serial* devices, since they send, or receive, information as a string of bits. The bits are sent one after the other at a very precise rate. This mode of transmission is useful when the I/O device is a long distance from

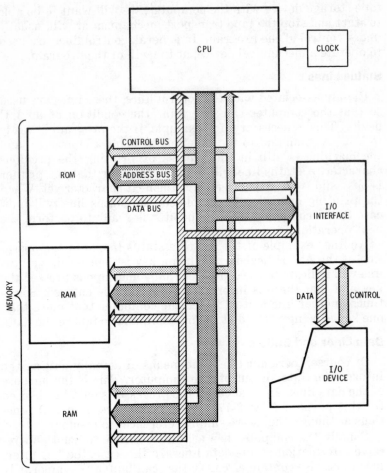

Fig. 2-17. I/O on the processor's busses.

the processor, and telephone lines are used to connect them. However, when the distance between the device and the computer is relatively short, the information can be transmitted as a complete word of data; all the bits in the word are sent simultaneously, with several wires being used to facilitate the transfer. This is called *parallel* I/O, because all the bits are transferred on several parallel lines simultaneously. An example of a parallel I/O device is the ASCII keyboard. When a key is pressed, the electronic circuitry associated with the keyboard interface generates the proper bit pattern for the character selected and puts it into a buffer as one word of binary data. The computer must then be notified that a key has been pressed and that there is a word of data in the buffer. Then, under the control of the program, the computer will read the word from the buffer and proceed to process it.

We can see that, in this case, there is very little need for synchronizing and timing, as compared with the previous examples of serial devices.

Interrupt Processing

As was discussed, there are many times when it is necessary to communicate with the computer, and each one of these cases requires the attention of the computer at some time or other in order to accomplish the transfer of information. In almost all cases, the information must be transferred under the control of the program. This would lead us to believe that the

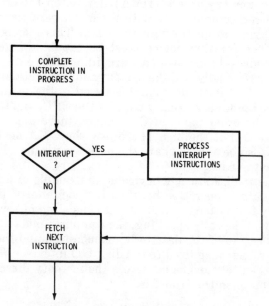

Fig. 2-18. Flowchart for interrupt processing.

computer would always be tied up trying to determine if some device was trying to send or receive information. This would be the case if it were not for the ability of almost every microprocessor to be very carefully interrupted.

One of the control lines leading into the CPU is used to interrupt the normal flow of the program being executed. (See Fig. 2-18.) When a signal is put on this line, the CPU will complete the particular instruction being executed. It will then be forced into a special section of the program which will make a note of the place where the interruption occurred and will analyze the various conditions of the system to determine what caused the interrupt. In this way, the computer can be working on some part of the program, and will process I/O only when the need arises and when a device causes an interrupt in the processing.

Direct Memory Access (DMA)

Most I/O devices require the attention of the CPU in order to communicate with the memory. For instance, if there is some information in the memory that we wish to be printed on the Teletype, the program must take care of transmitting every character to the I/O device. This will require many instructions each time a character is to be printed.

A *direct memory access* (DMA) device, on the other hand, is one that can communicate with the memory of the computer without having to go through the CPU. This means that the I/O interface for this device must be capable of generating memory addresses, as well as providing the data transfer. These devices usually use the system address and data busses, just as the CPU itself does. As discussed in the section on the CPU, these busses are greatly used by the CPU, and if they are to be used by other parts of the system, there must be provision for control of the bus. Therefore, the DMA device interface must also be able to share the busses with the CPU and to coordinate their use.

A magnetic disk storage device is an example of a DMA device. The data transmitted between the computer and the disk are usually formatted in large blocks consisting of several hundred words. Generally speaking, the computer must specify the memory location of the data to be transmitted and the number of words to be transmitted to the disk I/O interface. The interface will then take over and access the memory directly in order to accomplish the transfer.

SOFTWARE

One fact that cannot be overstressed is that, regardless of the complexity of the various electronic devices that the computer comprises, the computer is nothing more than an expensive toy unless there is a purpose for its existence and a program that will cause the purpose to be realized. It is the program, consisting of the individual instructions arranged in the order that they are to be performed, that will make the computer a useful tool to many.

There are many different types of programs and programming systems, all of which are referred to as *software*, as opposed to the electronic and mechanical elements of the computer, or the *hardware*. Some of these programs are used to accomplish a particular computing goal, such as to balance a checkbook or compute the area of circles. Other programs are used to operate the many I/O devices that we have discussed. The mechanical operation, as well as the transfer of the information between the computer and the device, is controlled directly by the program. Still other programs are used for special-purpose types of computing, for example, computing the square root of a number or doing any other arithmetic that the hardware (ALU) does not do itself. Sometimes these types of programs are referred to as *subroutines* because they are usually part of some larger program. For some given computer system, many programs may be collected, and all stored on magnetic disk. Then, one program is used to selectively "call in" any of these many programs that are to be used. Such a collection of programs is called an *operating system*, and if it happens to be stored on a magnetic disk, it is called a *disk operating system*.

Start-up Programs

The first consideration for the new computer user will be: "How do I get this thing to start?" Just applying the power to the computer will not cause it to immediately begin processing in the way that the user desires. There must be a program that initializes the system and then determines what the user's processing goals are. Once this is established, there must be a program that will set up the computer to perform the desired processing. A most convenient method of accomplishing this "start-up" is to have a program such as that described here, stored in read-only memory (ROM), which will automatically be executed when the computer is turned on.

Software Sources

It would be nice if manufacturers could program computers to suit the needs of the user. However, this would limit the usefulness of the computer, unless the user had many different programs available and they could be loaded into the computer easily. This may happen some day in the future, but for now, if you are planning to use a computer (especially a microcomputer), you had better be prepared to program it yourself. Of course, computer manufacturers claim to provide all the software that you would ever need. This is true, except that you have to be a *programmer* to be able to determine what you will be requiring. For this reason, the subjects of programming and software are not considered in any detail in this chapter. This information is given in Chapter 4.

chapter **3**

HARDWARE

Since the introduction of the first LSI microprocessor chip, the nature of hardware and of hardware logic design of digital systems has undergone vast and exciting changes. Although the design of digital systems has traditionally utilized large numbers of MSI (medium-scale integration) integrated circuits, such as counters, shift registers, gates, flip-flops, and multiplexers, connecting these chips together and debugging the design has remained a fairly complex and time-consuming practice. Since this problem is mainly due to the extremely large number of parallel interconnections between the MSI chips, it seems almost natural that the IC manufacturers would integrate all the MSI chips into one giant LSI chip. In combining the ICs into one package, the logic designers have been able to emulate some powerful computer functions in a space less than the size of a stick of gum and at a cost typically under $20 (Fig. 3-1). Yet, integrating MSI functions into one complex IC poses some interesting questions. For example, what type of computer structure should the chip emulate? The answer to this relatively simple question has produced a rich variety of microprocessor architectures, which has made the user's selection process complex.

The first microprocessor chip was a 4-bit device with a rather indirect computer structure. Since that time, microcomputers have become more like large general-purpose computers; instruction sets have grown in number and become easier to use, while speeds of operation have undergone vast improvements. Although there is no doubt that microprocessor technology will continue to improve, there will always remain

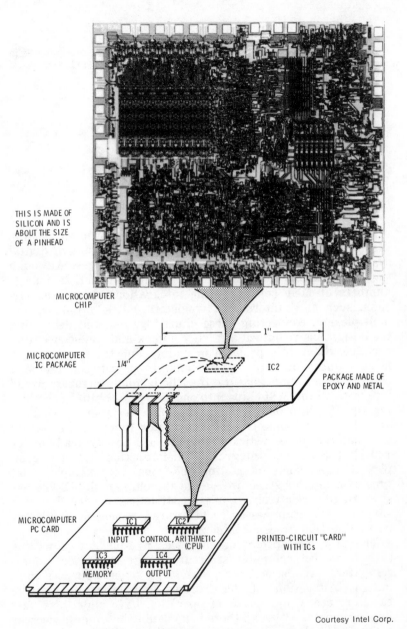

THIS IS MADE OF
SILICON AND IS
ABOUT THE SIZE
OF A PINHEAD

MICROCOMPUTER
CHIP

MICROCOMPUTER
IC PACKAGE

1/4"

1"

IC2

PACKAGE MADE OF
EPOXY AND METAL

MICROCOMPUTER
PC CARD

IC1
INPUT

IC2
CONTROL, ARITHMETIC
(CPU)

IC3
MEMORY

IC4
OUTPUT

PRINTED-CIRCUIT "CARD"
WITH ICs

Courtesy Intel Corp.

Fig. 3-1. How microprocessors are made.

the problem of interfacing these devices. Such an undertaking requires a good basic knowledge of the various hardware components that make up a working microcomputer, whether it is a product or development system. This is what this chapter is about.

Since the LSI chip is the device to which the entire system must interface, it makes sense to begin with a discussion of its requirements and operational characteristics.

CENTRAL PROCESSING UNIT (MICROPROCESSOR)

Fig. 3-2 illustrates a general-purpose microcomputer's structure. Inside the processor are the various registers described in Chapter 2. These components are not really available to the

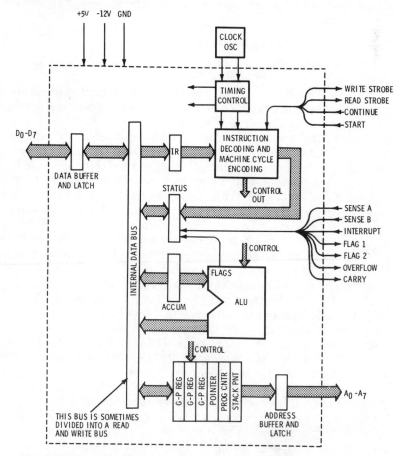

Fig. 3-2. Internal electronic structure of general-purpose microprocessor.

hardware interface but rather are controlled by the software program. The wide arrows indicate the fact that the data flow inside the processor involves a large number of parallel lines multiplexed between these various registers. The single-line arrows that are connected to the chip pins are control and interface lines, consisting of voltage input and ground for powering the IC, strobe information for catching data that are external to the chip at the proper time, status information on the internal states of the CPU, including the results of software programs, and "interrupt" pins which cause the internal hardware to interrupt the program and service an important event, then go back to the original program. There are also "start-up" pins for resetting all the internal registers to zero, "continue" inputs for stopping the program in midflight, and "sense" pins which let the computer measure some external event to determine its status.

Power, Timing, and Loading Rules

Let's examine the lines mentioned above in more detail, one at a time.

Power—The power requirements of most microprocessors are quite easy to meet. The usual voltage requirement is a 5-volt logic supply regulated to ±5 percent. Some of the earlier processors and some of the more cost-effective designs require a −7- to −12-volt bias supply, also regulated to within 5 percent. Power dissipation of the IC itself is relatively low, due to the fact that the monolithic structure is usually made of n- or p-channel MOS (metal-oxide semiconductor). A typical chip may dissipate a maximum of 1.2 watts, and typically produce only ¼ to ½ watt of power. The designer can find the actual numbers on the "common characteristics" data sheet for the particular microprocessor being examined. Usually, however, this amount of power is simply added to a list of system power requirements, which consist of the I/O device requirements, the interface dissipation, and the memory requirements. Typically the microprocessor will consume less than 20 percent of the total dissipation. (See Chart 3-1.) A good example of a microcomputer power supply suitable for handling 512 words of RAM memory, 256 words of PROM, the processor, and miscellaneous interfaces is shown in Fig. 3-3.

In addition to the system power-supply requirements, the designer may often opt to have his system run off a less-regulated supply (say 10 percent) and have a postregulator on each pc card in the system. These regulators can be simple three-terminal devices with no large filter capacitors required (except, of course, in the main supply). The advantage to this

POWER SUPPLY, + 5 V. HIGH-CURRENT –
REGULATED, +12 V, 40 mA. REGULATED, –7 V, 10-mA BIAS.

NOTE: i)   SINCE ALL CARDS USE 5V AND 1000 mA IS MAX AND 500 mA MIN, HEAT SINK FOR 1000 mA.
     ii)   + 12 V IN, +5 V OUT. 7-V DROP @ 1A = 7 W PER/CARD REGULATOR DISSIPATION MAX.
     iii) FOR A MAXIMUM HEAT SINK IDLE TEMP OF 35°C (10°C RISE ABOVE AMBIENT) @ 7 W,
          USE A 1.5°C/W SINK.

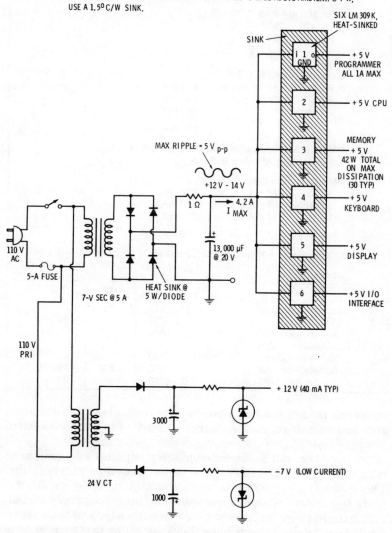

Fig. 3-3. Typical microcomputer power-supply schematic.

Chart 3-1. Typical Microcomputer Power-Supply Current Requirements

PROM Programmer: 575 mA @ 5 V, 40 mA @ 12 V

3 7447	70 mA ea. =	210 mA
3 Displays	84 mA ea. =	252 mA
Balance		100 mA
		562 mA

CPU: 500 mA @ 5 V, 10 mA @ −7 V

SC/MP	200 mA
Balance	300 mA
	500 mA

Memory: 1 A @ 5 V

ROM 8 8223	77 mA ea. =	616 mA
RAM 4 2101	70 mA ea. =	280 mA
Balance		100 mA
		996 mA

DMA Keyboard/Bus Multiplexers: 625 mA @ 5 V

9 TTL MSI	70 mA =	630 mA

DMA Keyboard Display: 1 A @ 5 V

5 8223	77 mA ea.	385 mA
5 Displays	84 mA ea.	420 mA
2 TTL	77 mA ea.	154 mA
		959 mA

I/O Interface: 500 mA @ 5 V; 50 mA @ 12 V; 20 mA @ −7 V

Summary:

	+5 V	+12 V	−7 V
Programmer (mA)	575	40	
CPU (mA)	500		10
Memory (mA)	1000		
DMA Keyboard/Bus (mA)	625		
DMA Keyboard/Display (mA)	1000		
I/O Interface (mA)	500	50	20
Totals (mA)	4200	90	30

approach is that the main power supply can be much cheaper, and additional regulators are required only as the system grows.

Some of the more efficient computer supplies use switching regulators instead of the static series pass-type of regulator. The switching regulator is more complex to build, as it converts the input voltage to a moderately high frequency signal, regulates it (which is easier now since it's ac), and then rectifies it back to dc. The problem, however, with these supplies is the transient switching pulses which can get into the memory or CPU and interfere with normal operation. Careful shielding can usually avoid this, but at a high cost. Since the series pass regulator is simple to use and troubleshoot, it makes good sense to utilize it in a microprocessor-based system where more complexity is not needed.

Good power-supply layout is extremely important here, and classic design rules should be followed to the tee. Ground traces should be made large and thick, and filter capacitors should be carefully distributed on the board to avoid contact with the heat developed by the regulator elements. Fuses are a must, and it will be well to fuse each individual pc board. Burning out an expensive microprocessor chip can be a terrible experience, especially when it represents more than 25 percent of the system cost. It would be good practice to check your ac outlet for improper voltage levels or noisy operation. Not all regulator designs can cope with large voltage spikes on the ac line. Monitoring the line for a couple of days with an oscilloscope will give some idea of the variations to expect. A digital voltmeter (dvm) would be excellent, and the numbers could be recorded for reference when you are choosing the regulator power supply. Fig. 3-4 illustrates some commercial microprocessor power supplies, including epoxy ±15-V modules; open-frame +5-V, 3-A supplies; and hefty autotransformer preregulators for transient protection.

The Clock—The clock requirements of various microprocessors range from as simple as a single capacitor (SC/MP and

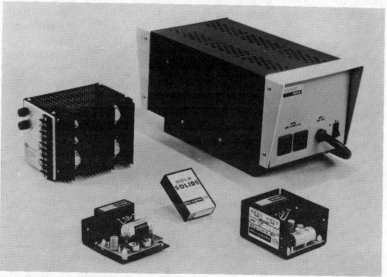

Courtesy Sola Basic Inds.

Fig. 3-4. Microprocessor power supplies.

MCS6502) connected to the chip pins, to dual-phase, nonoverlapping, controlled–fall-time, transistor driver circuits. The particular design depends on the way the manufacturer decides to implement the signals. In the more cost-effective designs, the clock should be extremely simple. In this case, the ideal clock is no clock (at least no external clock), and the manufacturer will either allow a capacitor to be connected to cause an internal circuit to oscillate at the desired frequency or use an external crystal which does the same thing but has a stability at least 1000 times that of standard-grade capacitors. The choice depends on how much stability is really needed; complex timing requirements are usually associated with complex high-speed interfaces. So, if the system is fairly simple, a crystal may not be necessary. Since all the various components in the microprocessor system use the clock as a reference, everything will drift at the same rate and only the overall time will vary. As soon as the microprocessor must interface with a device having its own clock circuit, using a capacitor for timing is asking for trouble.

The next level up in clock circuits is the simple crystal-controlled two-phase clock shown in Fig. 3-5A which is suitable for running an 8008 microprocessor. A crystal in the feedback loop of two NAND gates causes stable oscillation at 4 MHz. A dual flip-flop divides the oscillator signal by four, producing a stable 1-MHz clock. The final flip-flop works with two NAND gates to produce two nonoverlapping complementary waveforms. Fig. 3-5B shows the timing diagram for these signals.

At the other extreme of the spectrum are the requirements of the more complex microprocessors. Fig. 3-6 shows the typical clock waveforms for an n-channel MC6800 microprocessor. There are two clock signals which are called the $\phi1$ and the $\phi2$ clocks. These signals come from the same oscillator and are complementary and nonoverlapping. Since the inputs to the CPU chip are primarily capacitive (typically 110 to 160 pF maximum), the spec sheet is designed to handle the overshoot and undershoot produced from driving such a capacitive load. The clock specifications that constrain the clock the most are: the rise and fall times required to meet the pulse widths at the maximum operating frequency of 1 MHz, the nonoverlapping requirement, and the logic level requirements of $V_{ss} + 0.3$ volt and $V_{cc} - 0.3$ volt. The clock buffer circuit must handle the logic levels and the rise and fall time needs. The nonoverlapping requirement can be met by the design of control logic to drive the buffers. But in many systems, especially in the breadboard and evaluation stage, it may be desirable to have the flexibility to vary the system clock to test the effects on data

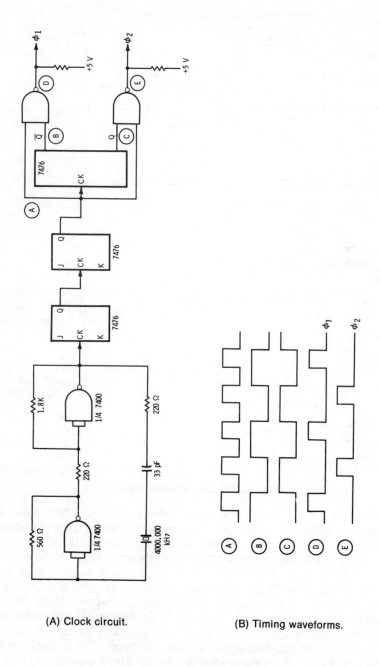

(A) Clock circuit.

(B) Timing waveforms.

Fig. 3-5. Crystal-controlled, two-phase, 1-MHz clock circuit.

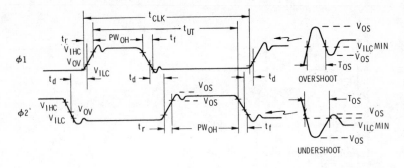

CHARACTERISTIC	SYMBOL	MIN	TYP	MAX	UNITS
Input High Voltage $\phi1$, $\phi2$	V_{IHC}	V_{CC}-0.3	—	V_{CC} + 0.1	V_{dc}
Input Low Voltage $\phi1$, $\phi2$	V_{ILC}	V_{SS}-0.1	—	V_{SS} + 0.3	V_{dc}
Clock Overshoot/Undershoot	V_{OS}				V_{dc}
Input High Voltage		V_{CC}-0.5		V_{CC} + 0.5	V_{dc}
Input Low Voltage		V_{SS}-0.5		V_{SS} + 0.5	
Input Leakage Current $\phi1$, $\phi2$ (V_{IN} = 0 to 5.25 V, V_{CC} = MAX)	I_{IN}	—	—	100	μa
Capacitance (V_{IN} = 0, T_A = 25°C, f = 1.0MHz)	C_{IN}	80	120	160	pf
Frequency of Operation	f	0.1	—	1.0	MHz
Clock Timing					
Cycle Time	t_{cyc}	1.0	—	10	μs
Clock Pulse Width					
(Measured at V_{CC}-0.3 V) $\phi1$	PW_{OH}	430	—	4500	ns
$\phi2$		450	—	4500	ns
Rise and Fall Times $\phi1$, $\phi2$ (Measured between V_{SS} + 0.3 V and V_{CC}-0.3 V)	t_r, t_f	5	—	50	ns
Delay Time or Clock Overlap (Measured at V_{OV} = V_{SS} + 0.5 V)	t_d	0	—	9100	ns
Overshoot/Undershoot Duration	t_{OS}	0	—	40	ns
Clock High Times	t_{UT}	940	—	—	ns

Courtesy Motorola, Inc.

Fig. 3-6. Clock waveforms for the MC6800.

throughput, to check real-time operation with interrupts, or to help diagnose a system timing problem. In these applications, a pair of crosscoupled monostable multivibrators with individual pulse width control, like the one shown in Fig. 3-7, can be used as the oscillator with the previously described driver circuits. The nonoverlapping clock is generated by the propagation delays through the multivibrators. Very small variations in pulse width will occur as the circuit elements are varied in this type of circuit. Since it will probably be necessary to drive other devices with the clock signal, it is good practice to buffer the master oscillator signal and provide a "clock out" signal on the clock circuit.

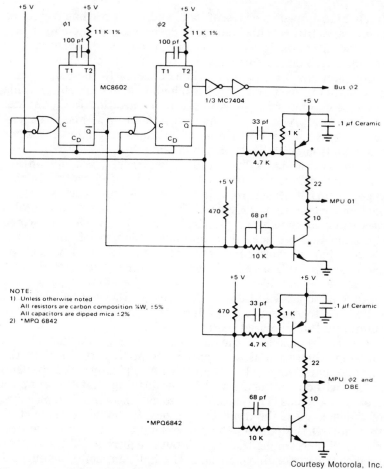

Courtesy Motorola, Inc.

Fig. 3-7. Typical clock circuit for driving the MC6800.

One final consideration for the clock circuit is the problem of cross talk from one clock line to another. This may occur with high-speed clocks and can be reduced by isolating the clock lines with ground lines and placing series damping resistors close to the drivers. The actual value of damping resistors should be on the order of 30 to 60 ohms and will depend on the particular circuit board layout. Rise time will be reduced with increasing resistance, and the ultimate value should not reduce this below the recommended values on the data sheet.

Fan-In and Fan-Out—Since most microprocessors are monolithic n- or p-channel MOS (mostly n-channel), it is necessary to carefully examine the signal buffering required to drive any particular load connected to the processor chip. MOS is a fairly high-impedance type of logic and therefore has restricted drive capabilities. This loading is designated as the chip's *fan-out* and is available as a specification on the data sheet. The cost-effective processors tend to require no buffering unless more than one TTL load is to be connected to the chip's pins. Translated into current, one TTL load is equal to 1.6 mA. This value of current may be exceeded by connecting too many devices to the processor. In many minimum systems, it is perfectly logical to have only one TTL load to drive; but in larger systems, it is quite likely that buffering will be required.

In some processors the output drive circuit is an open-drain transistor with the source connected to V_{ss} (+5 volts). In this type of output structure, a pull-down resistor is necessary at each output to allow driving CMOS or TTL devices. It is also necessary to switch the resistor from -12 to $+5$ volts when the same data pin is used as an input. This type of operation is slower than a "buffering" type of approach. In this method the open drains are used as current sources, and they drive a set of sense amplifiers which convert the current pulse to a voltage logic level suitable for the rest of the system. The only drawback to the sense amplifiers is the increased IC package count and the increased cost.

On the other side of the coin, the MOS high impedance is a blessing when used as an input. Since MOS gates draw in the microampere range (less than 2.5 μA typically), the limiting factor without buffering will be the loading that these inputs create on the bus. This is referred to as *fan-in* and is a measure of the leakage of the input transistors. It should be made clear that not all the pins on the processor have the same requirements. For example, the clock inputs require a TTL driver or special transistor drive circuit. The halt and continue outputs may be capable of driving low-power TTL or CMOS directly. If we are driving MOS inputs, not more than 10 such inputs may be driven simultaneously by a MOS output. This is because the maximum leakage of a MOS gate is a rather large variable and may be 10 to 100 μA. Thus, the typical fan-out when using MOS devices from the same family is on the order of 10 gates.

A third type of logic level found on most microprocessors is Tri-State. Developed initially by National Semiconductor, Tri-State has become a powerful tool for any application where many logic gates have to "talk" to each other over a common party line. In the regular mode, Tri-State acts identical with TTL; that is, a gate is one TTL load in, and can drive 10 TTL loads out. In the third state, the logic reverts to an open circuit. It is not a level halfway up but is physically disconnected from whatever line it was driving. This is accomplished by applying a logic signal to the gate's *output enable control*. Since the gate assumes a high-impedance state, it draws no current from the bus when it is not being used.

Most microprocessors' address and data pins are Tri-State gate outputs and are idle in the high-impedance open-circuit state. When the device is ready to transmit valid information to these pins, the outputs are selected by the processor and assume the desired TTL levels; when the information has been picked up by a receiving device, the output goes back to the high-impedance "off" state. Bus receivers, transmitters, and transceivers will be described in more detail when we consider the circuit organization for data transfers.

Construction Techniques—There are several methods available for building a microcomputer, ranging from purchasing a complete kit with all parts, boards, case, and instructions, to hand-wiring ICs on prototyping pc cards. Which method is best depends on the budget and plans of the builder. In between these two approaches are various alternative methods, such as wire-wrapping the minimum possible CPU and buying a commercial PROM programmer, or using a time-sharing assembler and a development system.

Kits are a neat way to go if you have access to about $500 to $1500. There is one cheaper form of kit, the so-called Educators and Learners, and this should be considered when all you want to do is develop some insights into how a certain microprocessor works. The kits are not without problems, however. One of these problems is getting a program into the computer. The most popular form of I/O media is paper tape, so you may have to get your hands on a Teletype with eight-level paper tape.

The next best method offers several unique advantages. This is the prototyping system, or the breadboard method, where we either wire-wrap, clip, solder, or plug ICs and components together at the schematic level. Simple "bootstrap loader" programs can be burned into PROM memory with a PROM programmer. The PROM programmer will be described in more detail after we cover PROMs in general, but basically it is a simple keyboard device for getting 1's and 0's permanently stored into the read-only memory.

There are several ways to breadboard your prototype system, including EL strips (Proto Boards), wire-wrap (the most popular), and expensive matrix plug boards.

EL strips (which go by other names also) are a matrix of tiny socket pins located on a strong nylon insulator (Fig. 3-8). The pins are arranged so an IC can easily be plugged into the matrix. Each pin of the IC will then have four tiny matrix

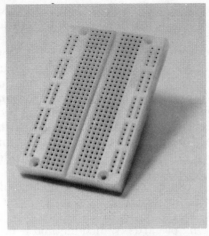

(A) Photo of EL strip matrix.

(B) EL strip internal connections.

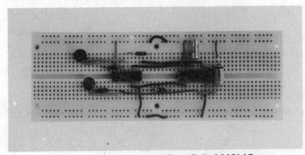

(C) EL strip for three to five digital MSI ICs.

Courtesy EL Instruments, Inc.

Fig. 3-8. EL strip matrix.

sockets available for inserting wires or components. A "general-purpose area" can be designated on the EL strip to enable the building of clock circuits, latches, drivers, etc. If a mistake is made, the component is simply unplugged (using very little force) and inserted in its proper location.

The only drawback to the EL strip is that, when used with digital logic of any complexity, the possibility of bad connections becomes a serious problem. Wires not properly inserted in the EL strip can come loose and go unnoticed. This can cause some strange results when the system is first fired up, and one can very well appreciate the use of carefully inserted connections.

Usually, the EL strip will be mounted on some sort of chassis which may also be used to hold a number of EL strips, power supplies, controls (if the system needs any), and various lights and displays (Fig. 3-9).

Fig. 3-10 shows a general-purpose microcomputer system designed for teaching microcomputer applications and utilization. It comes with a set of learning texts. The EL strips allow the system to be assembled in a fast, efficient manner, and the student can modify or add on outboard circuits with relatively little additional "mechanical" effort.

The other popular approach to a maximum flexibility system is the wire-wrap technique. In this case, special wire-wrap sockets are used with a Wire-Wrap gun (Fig. 3-11) that spins a wire around the posts of an IC socket. Such a "wrap" is solid and reliable, and if the wire isn't nicked in the process, it can take quite a bit of flexing without breaking. A thin, solid, solderplated (tinned) wire with thin Teflon insulation is usually used for making the wrap. The wire-wrap sockets are usually used in an epoxy pc board (Fig. 3-12) with holes punched in it every one-tenth of an inch and with edge connectors etched on one end of the card. The edge connectors may be soldered to, and in turn connected to, an edge connector receptacle. This brings the various connections on the board to the pins of the edge connector receptacle, and serves to anchor the board mechanically in place. Usually the board is plugged into a card cage which has many receptacles on it and room for several more pc cards. The backs of the receptacles are interconnected to form what is known as the *back plane*, which is nothing more than the final wiring harness. The back plane can be as sophisticated as snap-on ribbon cable connectors or as simple as more wire-wrap connections. The decision will depend on the final application.

If wire-wrap sockets are to be used, the builder should be acquainted with some of the techniques involved in building

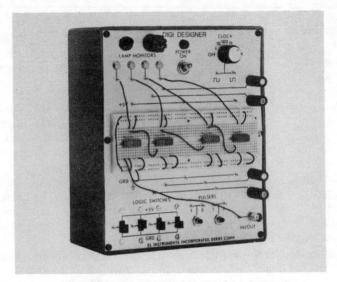

(A) Digital MSI EL strip development system.

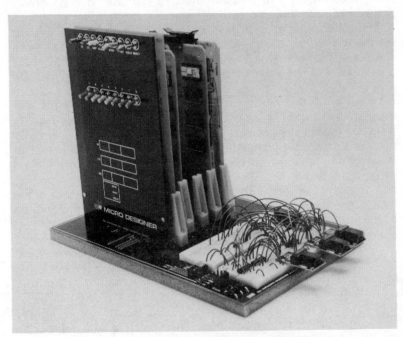

(B) LSI EL strip Micro Designer system.

Fig. 3-9. Chassis for EL strips.

circuits with them. One of the first subtle problems with wire-wrap breadboards is the problem of connecting components that are not in a dual in-line (DIP) package. A resistor, for example, poses an interesting insertion problem. If we try to squeeze it into a DIP socket, it will probably not fit too well (unless it's a small resistor). In other words, most of the discrete parts must be either made to fit into the DIP socket or soldered to a "header" pin which serves no other useful purpose than to provide a place to wire-wrap to. However, most

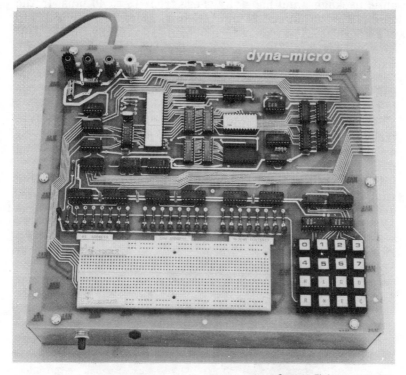

Fig. 3-10. LSI EL strip Dyna-Micro Designer.

good digital design at the prototype level will minimize the number of discrete parts. After all, the main reason for digital integrated circuits is to reduce the parts count. Of course, all circuits will require some discrete parts, such as the three-terminal regulators mentioned earlier. In this case, it is best to mount these parts with hardware (screws and nuts) and solder wires to their pins. The other ends of the wires are then attached with the Wire-Wrap gun to the necessary points.

One of the nice things about wire-wrap is the fact that an increasing number of important hardware devices are being made to plug into a 16- or 14-pin DIP socket. For example, all kinds of switches with tiny penpoint- or toothpick-actuated levers are available. Many of the seven-segment LEDs can fit in a 14-pin DIP socket, and there are different types of plugs that can connect to 16-conductor cable and be used as 16-pin connectors.

In mounting the LSI chips, extreme caution should be exercised. These chips are usually contained in fairly fragile ceramic packages, and have anywhere from 16 to 40 pins. In the case of the 40-pin and 24-pin LSI processors, it is advisable to use a special LSI socket, which is made specifically for the delicate packages and has a relatively low insertion pressure requirement.

Card cages, which are used for holding punched epoxy circuit boards, come in many shapes and sizes, and range greatly in price. A very simple card cage can be made with two pieces of 19-inch aluminum angle stock. The edge connector receptacles are used to give a shape to the card cage. The receptacles are simply attached to the angle stock with 6-32 screws and nuts.

Some excellent card cages are available commercially and range in price from $15 to $150 (Fig. 3-13). The differences are mainly in flexibility. Some cages come with special face-

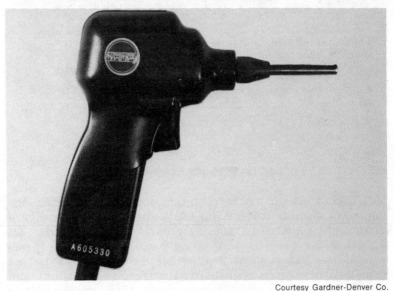

Courtesy Gardner-Denver Co.

Fig. 3-11. Wire-Wrap gun.

(A) Simple universal vector board.

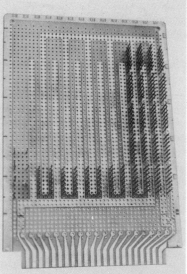

(B) Vector board with etched ground and V_{cc} traces.

(C) Microprocessor vector board accommodates 14-, 16-, 24- and 90-pin LSI DIPs.

Courtesy Vector Electronic Co., Inc.

Fig. 3-12. Epoxy pc boards for wire-wrap sockets.

(A) Simple vertical pc card holder.

(B) Card cage for vector boards.

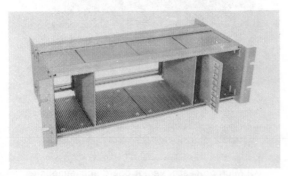

(C) Card cage with flexible card spacing.

Courtesy Vector Electronic Co., Inc.

Fig. 3-13. Commercially available card cages.

plates that can be attached to the pc card. This way, controls can be mounted on the panel so that they are physically close to the circuits. Another plus is the way in which these cages are easily rearranged; the edge connectors are usually movable and the card guides are either extruded slots or special individual movable slots. These allow the pc cards to accommodate parts of different heights on the board.

Input/Output Control

The operation of all microprocessors consists of repeatedly accessing or fetching instructions from the external program store and executing the operations specified by these instructions. These two steps are carried out by the internal hardware *microprogram,* which in essence is a dedicated ROM or PLA (programmable logic array, called the *decoder*) and an array of flip-flops, registers, and multiplexers inside the chip. This microprogram is similar to a state table specifying the series of states of system control signals necessary to carry out each instruction.

The Input/Output Cycle—Referring back to Fig. 3-2, which illustrates our general-purpose microprocessor, the fetch routine causes an instruction address to be transferred from the program counter register to the address bus, and initiates an input data operation. Various strobe signals occur, signaling the memory to provide the data at this address. When the instruction is provided on the data bus, the fetch routine causes it to be loaded into the instruction register (IR). The instruction operation code is now transformed into the address of the appropriate instruction-execution routine by the address generation logic. As a last step in the fetch routine, this address is loaded into the "microprogrammed" address register in the decoder, causing a branch to the appropriate instruction-execution routine.

The execution routine consists of one or more "microinstructions" to implement the functions required by the instruction. The number of microinstructions varies with the instruction. For example, the routine for a register ADD instruction would access the two registers to be added over the data bus (or operand bus if the architecture were different), cause the ALU to perform the ADD operation, load the carry and overflow flags from the ALU into the status register, and store the result in the specified register. The control logic interprets the microinstructions to carry out these operations.

The time required for each microcycle varies with manufacturers and devices, but it is usually on the order of 1 to 5 microseconds, with 2 being typical. The number of microcycles required for each microprocessor varies with the type of architecture chosen by the chip designers. Cost-effective types of processors will require many microcycles to complete an instruction, while the more sophisticated devices will require less. Typically, a slow processor will need 10 to 20 microcycles for a fetch and execute instruction, or about 20 to 40 microseconds. A more advanced type of processor may require only 4 or 5 microcycles, or 8 to 10 microseconds, to accomplish the same task.

Microprogram—The internal instruction decoders in a microprocessor chip are designed around ROMs or PLAs. This way the manufacturer can program the ROM and thus the instruction set. Fig. 3-14 shows how the ROM (in this case a

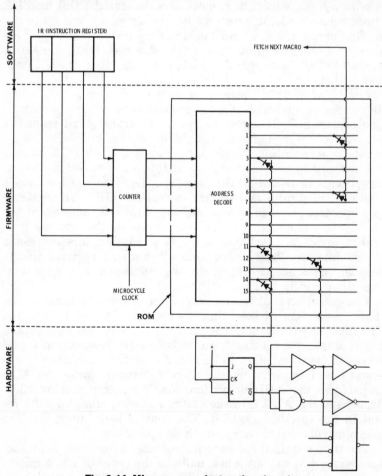

Fig. 3-14. Microprogram instruction decoder.

diode ROM for simplicity) interprets the instruction code into a hardware address that causes certain flip-flops and gates to operate (execute). This inner level of programming is called *microprogramming,* while the regular level of programming is referred to now as *macroprogramming.* These terms should not be confused with the terms used to describe the physical size of computers, as in minicomputers and microcomputers. Rather, this definition is useful only in illustrating the nature of the internal processor operation.

The internal clock is called a *microcycle clock* because it is used for driving the microsteps in an instruction. In this case it drives a counter that compares the incoming instruction from the IR to the count. When the value of the count reaches the address of the instruction, the counter stops and the ROM enables one particular set of diodes connected to that address. This, in turn, causes the hardware inside the chip to operate so as to complete the desired number of cycles for that particular instruction, and then to fetch the next macroinstruction into the IR.

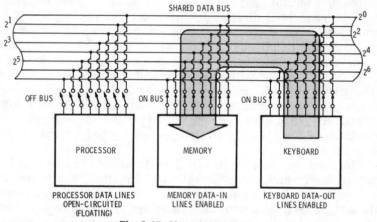

Fig. 3-15. Shared data bus.

Bus Access—The standard type of data transfer (fetch and store) among modern microprocessors is over a single 8- or 16-line I/O bus. This is usually a two-way type of bus system (called *bidirectional*). Most microprocessors use special control signals to allow many electronic devices to use this single bus without conflicts. Since the number of signal lines would double if separate data-in and data-out busses were used, the two-way system saves on wires and connections. Another refinement of microprocessor bus systems is a "shared" type of operation where, as shown in Fig. 3-15, digital I/O devices "hang" on a continuous eight-wire data bus. What makes such a bus system possible is the use of Tri-State bus transceivers. In the illustration, these are shown as switches which completely isolate all devices from the bus unless they are involved in a data transfer. For example, data from a keyboard may be entered directly into memory, without the use of the processor. Since the processor address and data pins are also Tri-State, it will not affect the bus unless it is actively sending out information or receiving data. The memory and keyboard thus share the bus, and the CPU is disconnected electrically.

Bus Transceivers—Since the system data bus is bidirectional, and the processor may sometimes be sending data and other times receiving data, some means of controlling the direction of the data on the bus is required. For example, consider a memory read (LOAD). The CPU addresses a word in memory and transfers it into the accumulator. In this operation, the memory will be "sending" and the CPU will be "receiving." To accomplish this, there are data output pins and data input pins. The output pins are connected to the low-impedance output stage of a MOS transistor. Therefore, these may be connected directly to the processor input pins. Now consider the opposite case, when the operation is a memory write (STORE). The CPU addresses a word in memory and transfers the contents of the accumulator into that location. Here, the processor will be sending and the memory receiving. The CPU chip will be presenting its low-impedance output transistor to the memory, but the memory still has its low-impedance output stage hooked up. This is bad news, and according to Ohm's law the two stages will try to burn each other out.

The solution is shown in Fig. 3-16. It shows one line of a bus transceiver, which has a "disable" or "direction" control on the driver section of the gate. Now when the CPU decides to send data, it issues a logic 0 to the transceiver's direction line, which effectively lifts the gate off the bus. The bus receiver is always connected (always listening), but the bus transmitter is turned on and off. The complete bus system includes the address bus as shown in Fig. 3-17. Here the CPU may be sending on the address lines, but it is never receiving on the address lines. Thus, there is no need for a transceiver on the address bus. However, we will probably have many devices *receiving* on the address bus. We must, therefore, make sure either that only one TTL load is being driven by the MOS processor, or that we use some form of buffering so that we don't care how many receivers are on the bus. This last approach is the most flexible but also requires the most parts.

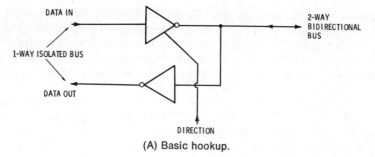

(A) Basic hookup.

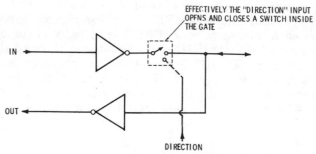

(B) Effect when CPU issues logic 0.

Fig. 3-16. Tri-State bus transceiver.

The modules shown in the figure provide the needed buffering and can be either memories or I/O devices which are addressed at specific memory locations by the processor.

The maximum number of devices on the address bus will be a function of the drive capability of the address driver buffer. For example, a 7404 hex buffer will drive up to 10 TTL loads. An 8T97 will drive up to 50 loads.

Note that this type of design is for a flexible, many-module-capacity system. In a processor designed for an "end product," the drivers and receivers may be absent or replaced with some type of latch on the memory or I/O device. In end-product low-cost design, as much hardware as possible is replaced with software. For example, if the input device requires that all its data be inverted for minimum parts count, the software program can include a simple routine that inverts all the bits in the data word before presenting the word to the output device.

Bus Control and Bus Request—One of the most interesting and advanced features of modern microprocessors is the ability to have more than one processor working on a single application. With several chips working on the same job, the overall time required to complete the job is shortened. An example of this type of design is a processor fitted with a mass storage device, such as a flexible disc. Since the disc requires a complex formatting circuit to organize the storage of data, the logic designer may choose to use a microprocessor for this purpose, to lower package count. But since the disc is to interface to another microprocessor, how do we effectively share the system bus between these two?

The solution is to use what is known as *bus request* and *enable input* and *enable output* functions on each microprocessor. Let's consider the flexible disc when data are to be read directly into the microprocessor's memory. Fig. 3-18 shows three control signals: bus request (BREQ), enable out (ENOUT), and enable in (ENIN). These signals appear on pins on each microprocessor. BREQ is actually an input and output type of circuit; ENIN is an input that stops all processor activity; and ENOUT is an output that indicates the processor is active. Bus request (BREQ) is used as a bus-busy and bus-request signal. When processor No. 1 is ready to use the bus (for example, if a memory fetch is to be executed), its

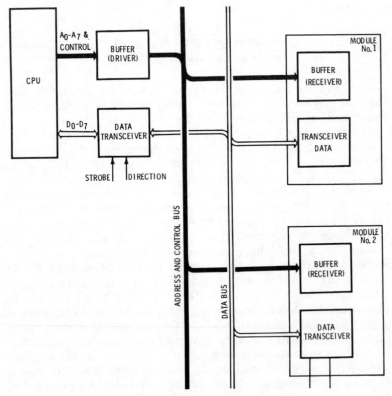

Fig. 3-17. Complete Tri-State system bus.

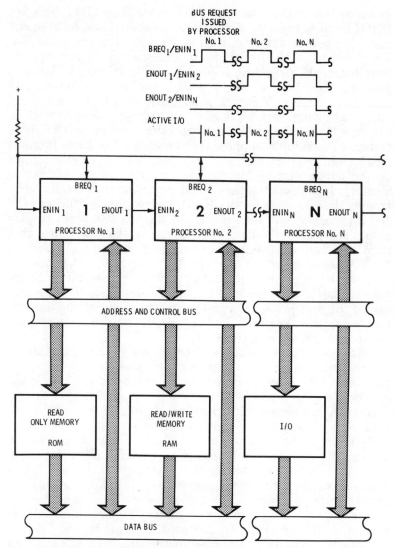

Fig. 3-18. Bus control and request among several processors.

BREQ line goes high. If the ENIN line on this processor is *not* low (lock-out condition), its ENOUT line will go low, signaling the other processors that this processor now has control of the bus. When the fetch cycle is complete, the BREQ input/ output line on the processor will go low. Since BREQ is tied back to the ENIN line, processor No. 1 ENOUT line will go high, freeing processor No. 2 to issue a bus request. If this processor needs the bus, its BREQ line will go high. Since its ENIN input is high, its ENOUT line is forced low, locking out any other processors down the line from it. Now processor No. 2 has control of the bus. If all processors issue a bus request simultaneously, the string is served on a priority-select basis—processor No. 1 first, No. 2 second, and so on. However, if processor number N issues a bus request and there are no others awaiting service, ENIN is high and the request is granted. Thus, any one of the processors can be a DMA controller. For example, suppose that processor No. 1 has just finished an instruction and now requires that a special program on the floppy disc be loaded into the processor's read/write memory. If we hook up the second processor as the DMA controller, then as soon as the No. 1 instruction is finished, the No. 2 processor will take control of the bus and begin to execute a search for the desired program on the disc. Since this may take many milliseconds (a very long time in CPU terms), the DMA controller has the bus only when the first processor is "in-between" instructions, that is, when it is doing an internal calculation or when it is waiting for an input. During this period the first processor is not using the bus, and the data on the floppy disc are transferred directly into the read/write memory, one word at a time.

Status and Flags—Status information appears as signals on the microprocessor pins. These signals indicate such things as the state of the internal registers, the results of arithmetic operations, or the type of instruction being executed. If microprocessors had an unlimited number of pins, *all* the vital status information could be brought out. However, since pins are at a premium, many designs use a strobe technique to put status information on pins that usually serve some other function. Here, let us first look at the simple status information that is available on the pins, and see how it is utilized. CPU flags are output gates that can be controlled by the program. For instance, suppose the programmer wanted to turn on a light at the end of the program. In this case, an LED is connected to the flag pin. The program reaches the end, puts a logic 1 on the flag bit, and the LED glows. Other uses of flags include turning I/O devices on and off, locking out interrupt signals, and any application where timing pulses are needed. A microprocessor may have from none to eight flags to manipulate.

"Sense" bits can be used to determine when an external device has completed an operation, such as when a printer has finished printing one character. These bits are nothing more than flip-flop states inside the CPU, which can be set, or reset, by signals applied to the CPU pins and then used by the program. For example, suppose an output device such as a printer has completed a print operation. It sends a logic signal to a sense pin on the CPU, setting the internal flip-flop. The CPU keeps checking this bit in a programmed loop (i.e., it checks it over and over). When it finds that the bit has been set, the CPU branches to a routine that resets the flip-flop (so that the next time the event occurs it will be ready) and completes the next series of instructions.

Of course, sense information must be checked constantly by the processor to see if it has changed, which can easily tie up the entire processing time. Often it is desirable to have the external event actually signal to the processor when it occurs, freeing the CPU to operate on another job. This technique is known as interrupting the processor, or more commonly as an *interrupt*.

Interrupts—The classical form of interrupt uses a pin on the CPU called the interrupt sense bit. This pin is connected with an internal hardware circuit which performs a rather complex but useful purpose when activated. Assuming the microprocessor is running, a signal on the interrupt pin will cause the current instruction to finish executing, and then will take the program counter value and swap it with a special register containing the address of the beginning of the interrupt program. The interrupt program begins execution. If the information contained in the CPU registers at the time the interrupt occurred is valuable, the first thing the interrupt program must do is save all the important registers in memory locations. Afterwards, these values can be put back in the CPU, the program counter content swapped back with the special interrupt register, and program execution resumed where it left off.

Fig. 3-19 shows a flowchart for a typical interrupt procedure. The only problem with this interrupt system is that it cannot service more than one interrupting device without first going through a special routine that figures out which device requested the interrupt. In other words, since there is only one interrupt pin, there will be only one interrupt subroutine. Ideally, we would have other pins that would allow a number of subroutines and a number of interrupting devices on the same processor. In the more advanced processors, there are several types of interrupts and more than one interrupt pin on the CPU. For example, on the MC6800, the interrupt request (IRQ) causes the CPU to finish the current instruction, set an interrupt mask bit, and then stack all the internal registers in an area of memory reserved for them. Next, it loads the program counter with two bytes of address which it gets from another dedicated area in memory. This is the address of the beginning of the interrupt subroutine that the user associates with this pin.

Another interrupt input on the MC6800 called NMI, or non-maskable interrupt, is recognized as soon as the pin changes to a logic 0. In contrast, the IRQ must first set the interrupt mask bit for allowing the processor to sort out which device on the pin came first. The NMI is similar to the IRQ but goes to a different location to pick up the address of the interrupt subroutine. Reset, or RES, is an interrupt used for starting up

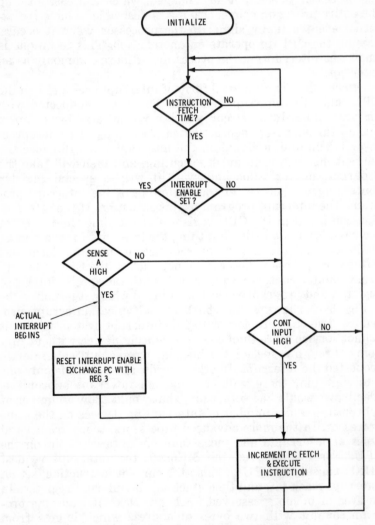

Fig. 3-19. A simple interrupt sequence.

the processor and puts the interrupt vector on the address bus for this particular interrupt. No status is stacked, however, as the interrupt program is used to initialize the CPU.

A final type of interrupt is the software interrupt (SWI). It is similar to an IRQ except that it is initiated by an instruction in the program. It is useful for inserting breakpoints and as a debugging aid.

Interrupts With Priority Control—Often it is necessary to service interrupts on some sort of priority basis, that is, a method that assigns levels of importance to the particular device and allows a more important device to be serviced first. The circuit that accomplishes this task is the priority encoder circuit. All of the devices are connected to the priority encoder, which in turn provides the interrupt to the processor, indicating which device requires attention. If another device signals for service at this time and it has a higher level of priority assigned to it, the encoder will stack all the current registers, place the new vector in the program counter, and branch to the new interrupt location. Such priority circuits are necessary when the processor cannot take the time to calculate which device was requesting service on a polling basis. A polling method simply checks a status flag on each interrupt device until it finds the one issuing the request. The order in which it polls establishes the priority. This approach uses less hardware but requires more software.

Strobed Status Information—This serves mainly to provide bit-by-bit information on the internal state of the processor as it runs. Although extra pins could have been added to simplify this feature, extra pins have a gross effect on the cost of the chip. Fig. 3-20A shows a typical input/output sequence for a low-cost processor. Status information, along with 4 bits of address, is strobed onto the data bus, just before the data appear. This is referred to as the valid I/O status time. The status information in this case is a *read cycle flag*, which tells us that the data input cycle is starting; an *instruction fetch flag*, which tells us that the first byte of an instruction is being fetched; a *delay flag*, which tells us that the beginning of a programmed delay cycle is starting (that is, the second byte of the delay instruction is being fetched) ; and a *halt flag*, which tells us that a HALT instruction has been executed. That information requires that four bits of the data bus be sent out. Since the other four bits of data bus are available, some chips use them as address extension bits. In this example, the address width of the microprocessor pins is 12 bits, for a maximum address of 4096. The four bits on the data bus, available during the address strobe time, contain the "page" information for selecting one of 16 possible 4096-byte pages of memory. For the first 4096 bytes of memory, we can simply use the microprocessor's address pins directly. The remaining four bits of information must be latched during any memory read or write. Thus, the processor appears to get 64,000 bytes of address range on 12 address pins!

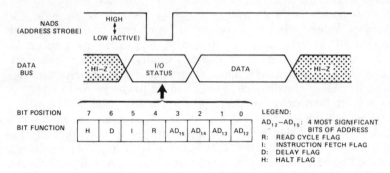

(A) Data bus at address strobe time (SC/MP).

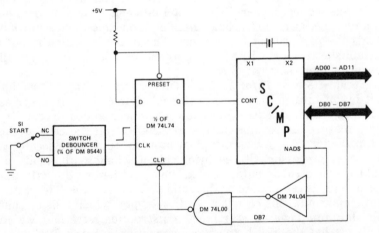

(B) Using the H flag to generate a programmed HALT (SC/MP).

Courtesy National Semiconductor Corp.

Fig. 3-20. Strobed status and programmed HALT.

Start-up and Halting—Starting and stopping the processor are accomplished by various hardware functions inside the chip. For example, all microprocessors have a "reset" input pin. When the reset input is made low, it aborts any processor operation. When returned from low to high, it initializes all internal registers, and the next instruction is fetched from memory location 1. (Naturally, the instruction at this address must be the beginning of a routine that starts the processor on its merry way.)

An interesting way to *stop* a microprocessor is shown in Fig. 3-20B, where a flip-flop and NAND gate are used to generate a manual or programmed halt. A programmed halt is one initiated in the software program, as opposed to a manual halt initiated by a mechanical switch. The Q output of the flip-flop drives the CONT input of the processor, which, when high, allows the next instruction to be fetched and the computer to run. When low, it halts the processor prior to the next instruction fetch cycle. Two things control this flip-flop: a start switch that the user controls for manual start and stop, and a NAND gate monitoring bit D_7 of the data bus. The NAND gate is NANDed with the strobe signal NADS, which occurs when valid status is available on data bus. The NAND gate then drives the clear input of the flip-flop latch. As long as D_7 is not high (halt flag not set), the NAND gate keeps the clear input high and the processor runs. (The start switch can be momentarily closed to stop or start the processor manually.) When the H flag is set by the HALT instruction, the clear input of the latch goes low, which sets the Q output low and stops the processor. Since the HALT instruction is all zeros (00000000), an accidental jump to an empty area of memory will read in all zeros and cause a safe programmed halt.

Another example of using the status information in a strobed system is the logic for single-cycle and single-instruction control of the processor. In Fig. 3-21, switch S1 sets the mode of the processor to single instruction if the user wishes to have an instruction fetch, execute, and wait, or to single cycle if only a fetch and wait are desired.

When the RUN switch, S2, is momentarily set to its NO contacts, the RS flip-flop sets and clocks a latch driving the NHOLD input to the processor. NHOLD is an input that when high has no effect, and when low causes the processor input or output cycle to extend. If NHOLD is dropped low during a memory input or output cycle, it will freeze the data and address information on the chip pins, and the CPU will remain stopped until the pin goes high again. The CONT input of the processor is driven by another latch. In this case, CONT allows cycling the processor through an entire instruction, rather than just the fetch portion as the NHOLD circuit allows. And finally the NADS signal, which occurs during the address strobe time, is used to reset the two flip-flops for the beginning of a new cycle.

On some of the more advanced processors, the strobed status information is much richer in content. For example, the 8080 sends out 10 status signals concerning the input/output cycle;

these tell if the cycle is an instruction fetch, memory read, memory write, stack read, stack write, input, output, interrupt, halt, or interrupt while halted. However, the 8080 also requires a more complex latch to utilize the status information.

CPU Comparison

In the preceding chapters we have alluded to the slight differences in microprocessors and tried to be general in our discussion. Now we are going to explore the differences between one chip and another. At this writing there are over 50 different microprocessor chips on the market and over 100 different versions of these chips packaged in a computer system. Although it's quite probable the microprocessor field will become even more diverse, there seems to be a reduction process occurring, in that the differences between processors are dwindling. In fact, since the introduction of the first 4-bit machine, a standard of 8 bits has become the popular size for a data word, and 16-bit addresses are typical. Simplified input/output instructions that treat an I/O device as a memory location are a trend. Internal "on-chip" clocks to simplify timing require-

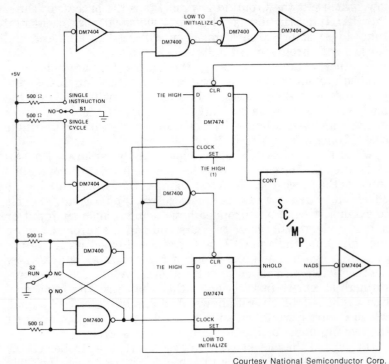

Courtesy National Semiconductor Corp.

Fig. 3-21. Single-crystal/single-instruction control (SC/MP).

ments, and Tri-State output structures that allow easy peripheral interfacing are on the increase.

There are five important areas to examine when evaluating a microprocessor: the instruction set, the number of addressing modes, the speed of execution, the interrupt technique, and, finally, the size of the address and data word. Fig. 3-22 illustrates a "universal" CPU block diagram which we will use for our comparisons. It contains all the important registers of a typical microprocessor, the clock circuit, and the system busses.

Instruction Set—Although we will cover this topic in finer detail in the programming section, for now it is important to realize that there are some dramatic instructional differences among today's microprocessor devices. Most of the squeezes the manufacturers make are to simplify the logic inside the chip, reduce the number of pins, and keep the cost of the mask to a minimum.

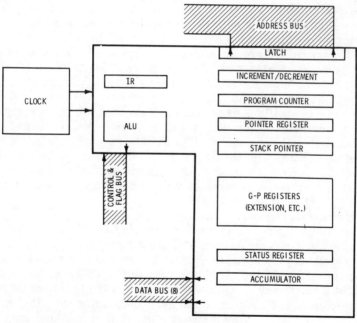

SPECIFICATIONS:
NUMBER OF INSTRUCTIONS
MIN & MAX INSTRUCTION EXECUTION TIME (SPEED)
NO. OF ADDRESSING MODES
INTERRUPT TECHNIQUE
SIZE OF DATA WORD
SIZE OF ADDRESS

Fig. 3-22. CPU reference diagram.

The later generations of microprocessors have evolved quite complete instruction sets with rather sophisticated mathematical and logical instruction modes. Most have ALUs that add and subtract, that allow double-precision arithmetic, binary-coded decimal (bcd) arithmetic, as well as signed and unsigned binary and two's complement (see Appendix A). The logical functions of the ALU are also high-powered, including all types of ANDs, ORs, exclusive ORs, rotates, shifts, and complements. Clearly, the absolute number of instructions in the set tell us something about the power of the processor. The low-cost type of processors may have anywhere from 30 to 40 instructions, while the more sophisticated types have upwards of 75 to 200 instructions.

Addressing Modes—Since the microprocessor spends much of its time addressing memory or peripherals, it makes sense to have a large number of addressing instructions. The low-cost microprocessors are limited in this respect and will usually allow a maximum of four types of addressing: *PC relative,* where the address is obtained from the current address in the program counter and the displacement located in the operand field; *indexed,* where the address is obtained from some internal pointer register and the displacement is added to it; *immediate* addressing, where the second byte of the instruction is used as the data; and, finally, *auto-indexed,* which provides the same capabilities as indexed, except that the pointer register is incremented or decremented by some value after it is used. Although this sounds like more than enough addressing modes, it turns out that even more sophisticated modes are available in the higher-level processors, and that we can do more with them. These modes will be described in more detail in the next chapter.

Execution Time—The ultimate speed of any processor depends on so many variables that deciding which is the fastest can be quite a complex job. The reason for this is that execution speed is job dependent; one processor may complete a certain program faster than another, but a different program might turn the tables. One easy way to get an idea how fast the computer runs is to pick a standard instruction, one that will be used in your application quite often, and see how long it takes to execute according to the particular manufacturer's specification sheet. (The latter may also be referred to as the Instruction Set Summary Card.) The trick to this method is discovering how many cycles the instruction requires.

Often the number of cycles is given in the summary card listed under the character N or $\wedge$. This number is then multiplied by the machine cycle time to obtain the speed of the instruction. (Machine cycle time is usually not the same as clock cycle time. Many clock cycles make a machine cycle.) In the MC6800, the lock time *is* equal to the machine cycle time (1 MHz). An "indexed load" requires 5 MPU machine cycles. Therefore, this instruction takes five times 1 microsecond, or 5 microseconds, to execute.

The SC/MP processor uses a slightly different formula to come up with the cycle time. In this case, the oscillator is internal and a capacitor sets the frequency. The machine cycle, however, is two times this number. Thus, for a 1-microsecond clock time the cycle time is 2 microseconds. An indexed load on SC/MP requires 18 microcycles, and therefore the instruction requires 18 times 2 microseconds, or 36 microseconds. Thus, we can begin to see the difference in execution time required by these two devices to move a byte of data into the accumulator. Since this is something we may do often, we should ask ourselves if the SC/MP, which is more than five times slower than the 6800, is a worthless machine. Of course, the answer is: Absolutely not. We often find that our application can be handled in a slightly different way so that the time requirements are not so formidable. Or, we may find that a multiprocessor approach will be more effective. Regardless, one should reserve judgment until *all* the various details of the Instruction Set Summary Card have been examined.

Interrupt Technique—The manner in which each manufacturer chooses to implement the interrupt feature on his processor has a direct bearing on the ability of the device to handle complex I/O operations. For example, the first processors lacked even a simple interrupt technique, making it very difficult to have an I/O device signal to the CPU that it had completed its task. Some later generations of processors have a very advanced interrupt technique. At least six levels of vectored interrupt may be provided with the addition of three or four pins.

Size of Address and Data Word—This is perhaps the largest variable among microprocessors, with each company making different sizes for different requirements. The early processors were all 4-bit data-word machines, and were adequate for handling bcd arithmetic and simple calculatorlike jobs. The size of the data word has a direct bearing on the "resolution" of the processor, and 4 bits provide for one part in 16. Arithmetic in a 4-bit machine is done on a digit by digit basis, usually on binary-coded-decimal digits (see Appendix A). With an 8-bit data word, we get better resolution (one part in 256) and the arithmetic process is simplified. The 16-bit machine gets one part in 65,636 but, of course, requires more pins to implement.

The size of the address word gives us a good indicator of the addressing range of the CPU. A 4-bit machine usually has to send out an address in 4-bit chunks, which makes programming rather tedious. Three chunks give 12 bits, or 4096 words. With the 8-bit machine, addressing is usually accomplished in two chunks. The 16-bit machine offers the best addressing range of all, needing only one word to cover the entire 64K of memory. Although the trend is to use 8-bit data words and 16-bit address words, it is probable that a 16-bit standard will eventually occur.

Now that we have a better idea of what each of the five microprocessor parameters means, let's take a closer look at individual processors. We will consider the chips in their chronological sequence, covering the five important parameters, as well as some of the peculiarities of the chip design.

4004—The 4004 was the early bird in the field. Introduced in 1973, it is the 4-cylinder model-A processor, in a 16-pin DIP, that started the ball rolling. Originally designed for a Japanese calculator, the 4004 almost emulates a general-purpose computer in the sense that it can be programmed as a different type of calculator. Its main drawback is the difficulty in actually programming it. A 4004 has a 4-bit data word and uses a 4-bit bidirectional bus to send out not only data, but chunks of address. The memory chips are designed to latch the data from the CPU, and thus the CPU will not work with standard memory. Yet with all these drawbacks, designers could see that the chip family offered cost-effective and interchangeable calculator designs.

Inside the 4004 is a 12-bit program counter and an 8-bit instruction register. The 4004 has a total of 45 instructions and a 10.8-microsecond cycle time. Loading from memory into the accumulator requires first sending out three 4-bit chunks of address, which takes a two-word instruction. Thus, 21.6 microseconds is consumed in setting up the address. The returned data are stored in an internal register. Next, the accumulator is actually loaded with the contents of this register, which takes a one-word instruction, or 10.8 microseconds. Thus, the total time is 21.6 + 10.8, or 32.4, microseconds.

The interrupt on the 4004 is called TEST and isn't really an interrupt. The TEST is really a sense bit and can be tested periodically with a JUMP instruction. Thus, interrupts on the 4004 are ruled out, unless some complex hardware is added outside the chip. Calculators, however, don't really require interrupts to function, so any calculatorlike job can be implemented.

4040—Although the 4040 (Fig. 3-23) didn't come next, historically speaking, it is a revealing chip to examine in the light of the 4004, its little brother. The 4040 is functionally equivalent to the 4004 and upward-compatible. Fourteen new instructions are added for a total of 60 instructions. These additional instructions enhance the 4004's usefulness and show what a general-purpose CPU should approach. First the ALU was improved, and logical and compare instructions were added to it. Seven levels of subroutine nesting were added to the 4004 basic addressing instructions. Eight more pins were added, making the unit a 24-pin LSI chip. Perhaps most important, an interrupt enable instruction and interrupt acknowledge input and

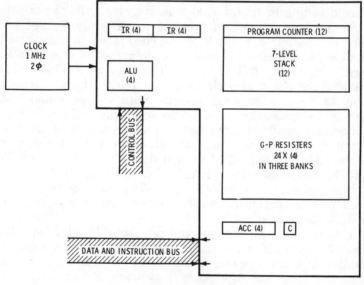

Fig. 3-23. 4040 4-bit CPU.

output instructions were added, along with the internal hardware structure needed to process the interrupt. A HALT instruction was finally added to the instruction set so that the CPU could easily be stopped. Also, the carry bit was brought out to an external pin. However, the bus and address capabilities remained the same, still requiring much multiplexing and indirect programming. These drawbacks notwithstanding, the 4040 has been used in everything from incremental tape recorders to turkey-weighing machines. Its primary advantages are low cost, a moderate-size package, and a well-developed chip set for input/output control. Its main disadvantages are inability to work with standard memory and its small-size data word.

8008—Although the 4004 IC chip got the ball rolling, the 8008 caught the attention of an even larger group of enthusiasts, particularly because it was the first 8-bit machine on the market (hence the 8 in 8008). The 8008 manages to get all the important registers, data, I/O, and status pins in a single 18-pin DIP package. The 8008 also has a combined data and address bus. A considerable amount of multiplexing is required to separate the data and address information. The chip can address up to 16K bytes of memory, and does so by sending out two bytes of address information which must be latched by the user (contrary to the more recent chips). The secret of the 8008's small package is that the design requires external hardware decoding of its internal machine cycle, and the latching of the various portions of these cycles. There are three state lines (S_1, S_2, and S_3) which are decoded into five time periods. Each 8008 instruction requires some amount of these; an I/O cycle requires the full five steps. The fastest 8008 has a 12.5-microsecond machine cycle time. An indexed load instruction requires first setting up a register with an upper and lower byte that points at the memory location. Since the upper byte is a maximum of 6 bits, the range of addressing is 14 bits wide, which gives an address range of 16K bytes. The remaining bits of the address are latched to provide status information. The actual indexed load from RAM takes three instruction bytes, and, therefore, three times 12.5, or 37.5, microseconds. This is close to the same time as the 4004, which takes three times 10.8, or 32.4, microseconds.

A minimum 8008 system requires about 10 additional MSI ICs. This in itself is not justification to avoid the 8008, as its small 18-pin package size means extremely low cost. In addition, the 8008 has a high-level systems language compiler called *PL/M*. In fact, it was the first processor to offer this capability. This type of programming allows the user to develop an 8008 task on a time-shared terminal (at a nominal monthly cost). The same terminal "outputs" 8008 machine code for running the microprocessor. The user then takes the machine code (usually on paper tape) and enters it into the 8008 system. Obviously, this speeds up the application development cycle for the 8008, which is probably why it became the microprocessor standard.

Software people were quick to recognize the language potential of the 8008, and it wasn't long before programming manuals from consulting houses became available. These manuals enlightened many engineers about the value of programming, as did the proliferation of companies teaching courses on how to utilize the 4- and 8-bit machines.

About this time, *Radio-Electronics* magazine carried an article about the first hobbyist computer, called the Mark 8. It was a simple and cost-effective design with excellent documentation. The Mark 8 was later modified, and today remains one of the best-known processors around.

Like the 4040, the 8008 has the barest of interrupt systems, and suffers from this shortcoming in the more complex applications. The answer to this problem was right around the corner as 8008 users discovered the upgraded 8080.

8080—The 8080 (Fig. 3-24) was the first really high-powered CPU to hit the market. It has a machine cycle time of 2 microseconds, which is about five times faster than the 8008. In addition, the 8080 has a 16-bit program counter that allows addressing up to 64K bytes of memory. It can do decimal, binary, and double-precision arithmetic, and has 78 basic instructions.

The price of all this sophistication is the addition of 22 more pins to the old 8008, making the unit a 40-pin LSI ceramic IC. The extra pins are used for addressing (16), data in and out (8), interrupt, reset, and three power supplies (4).

An indexed load instruction requires three bytes of instruction. The three bytes set up all the internal counters needed to

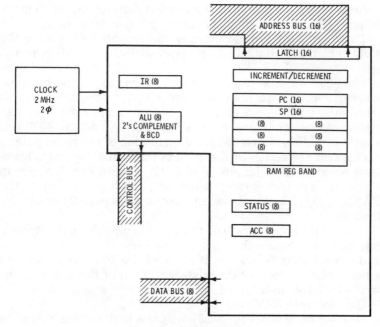

Fig. 3-24. 8080 8-bit CPU.

point to the proper memory location; no latching is needed. The instruction takes three machine cycles to execute, or 6 microseconds total. This is quite fast by 8008 standards.

In addition, the 8080 has a rich mix of ALU instructions, including rotates, shifts, compares, exclusive ORs, and more. It can do decimal subtraction or addition, which allows simple and easy bcd interfacing.

The 8080 contains six 8-bit general-purpose working registers and an accumulator. The six general-purpose registers may be addressed individually or in pairs, providing both single- and double-precision operators. Arithmetic and logical instructions can set or reset four flags.

The 8080 uses an external stack feature in which any portion of memory may be used as a last-in/first-out stack to store or retrieve contents of the accumulator, flags, program counter, and all six of the general-purpose registers. A 16-bit stack pointer controls the addressing of this external stack. This gives the 8080 the ability to handle multiple-level priority interrupts by rapidly saving and restoring processor status. Also, it provides almost unlimited subroutine nesting. Ultimate control of the data and address bus is provided by a HOLD input pin on the 8080. This pin forces the processor to suspend operation, and drives the busses into a high-impedance state. This permits ORing the bus with other controllers for direct memory access (DMA) operations, or multiprocessor operation.

There are a total of 512 directly addressable I/O ports in the 8080, which are controlled by a special I/O instruction in the set.

The 8080 was the second microprocessor to hit the hobbyist market and, due to its more sophisticated structure, it was more successful. Today there are probably more 8080 computer systems in use than any other single device, and the 8080 has almost established a record for distribution of microcomputers.

One real attraction of the 8080 is the availability of a high-level programming language (PL/M) and an excellent group of assemblers and editors. Moreover, the first version of the BASIC programming language appeared especially made for the 8080.

From this point onward, the microcomputer field expands considerably. Nine other processors were introduced during, and immediately following, the rise of the 8080, and each had a particular reason for its existence. Of all of these, one of the most attractive in terms of its simplicity and ease of utilization is the Motorola MC6800.

6800—The 6800 (Fig. 3-25) was the first serious threat to the 8080 market. The secret to the 6800's success was not due solely to its being a better processor. Rather, its success was due to the fact that the designers of the 6800 didn't stop at the CPU, but went on to develop a complete family of ICs. The 6800 family contains, for example, an LSI parallel interface adapter (PIA) that allows the microprocessor to send and receive 8-bit parallel binary data to two independent I/O devices. The LSI device has all the necessary logic functions needed for parallel interfacing to remote devices, and eliminates a large number of MSI packages. The simplicity of this "family" approach is that almost no extra circuits are required to create a working system.

The complete family contains a CPU, PIA, ACIA (asynchronous interface adapter), modem (low- and high-speed), clock, and various bus interface logic ICs.

As a processor, the 6800 has photofinishes in benchmarks with the 8080. As for size, the chip has the same 8-bit data word and 16-bit address range as the 8080. The bus system is completely Tri-State, with inputs for causing the bus to switch into a high-impedance state, or for enabling it at the proper time.

The instruction set of the 6800 looks exceedingly simple, except for the fact that there are seven different types of address-

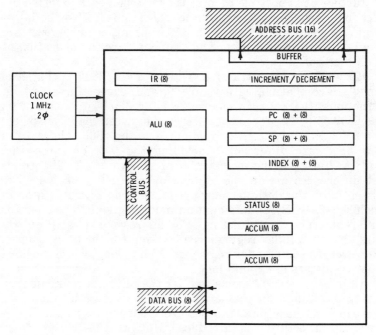

Fig. 3-25. 6800 8-bit CPU.

ing modes. Learning to use all these can take a while, but a little study reveals some of the 6800's power. The addressing modes include: direct, relative, immediate, indexed, extended, implied, and accumulator. The flexibility of the interface needs of the 6800 is most likely due to its close resemblance to the Unibus® concept, where all the various peripheral devices share the bus. Each device on the bus is treated by the CPU as a valid memory address. Therefore, all the memory reference instructions of the 6800 are also used for communicating with peripherals and remote devices. Such a straightforward approach relaxes the interface requirements for both software and hardware designers.

The problem of interrupting the processor while it is in a program, and the subsequent problem of distinguishing between many external interrupting devices, is simplified by the availability of four different interrupt pins on the 6800. Each of these serves a different function in changing the course of the operation. Among them is the nonmaskable interrupt, NMI. This pin, when brought low, causes the 6800 to automatically save five different registers in a specific location in memory, and then to vector to another specific location in memory containing the starting address of the interrupt subroutine.

Further, it is possible to have the 6800 poll each external device in a daisy chain to determine which one effected the interrupt. Interrupts that suspend MPU operation until reset are available for single-cycling and single-instruction operation of the processor.

6502—The most attractive feature of the 6502 is that it is software compatible with the 6800, and, except for a few instructions, the programs developed for 6800 systems run on the 6502 chip. The foremost difference between the ICs is price; the 6502 costs about a third as much as the 6800. There are a few hardware differences, including the lack of three-state address lines and the inclusion of an on-chip clock. The greatest differences are in the addressing capability of the 6502. Essentially, the designers dropped the second accumulator in the 6800 (ACCB) and made it an index register to be used for different types of addressing. For addressing arrays and tables, the extra index register is a blessing for the programmer. However, the 6800 index register is 16 bits long, while the 6502 index registers are 8 bits long.

All in all, the 6502 seems to offer the ultimate refinement in a single-chip microprocessor. But, while all the 8-bit machines were making headlines, another processor with a radically different architecture was introduced. Hosting a 16-bit data word and an especially flexible interrupt structure, the PACE chip from National Semiconductor Corp. kicked off the first of the 16-bit microprocessors.

PACE—The PACE (Fig. 3-26) differs from the previous designs in that all the address and data bits are issued from a single 16-bit–wide port on the chip. External circuitry, in conjunction with PACE state information, latches and picks up the address or data bits from the same bus. Since the address and data share the same bus, the external structure and pc layout of the system are simplified. Since the processor uses 16-bit data words, resolution of 1 part in 65,636 can be obtained. Only a single memory read is needed to address up to 64K, whereas in the smaller 8-bit machine two bytes of data must be read sequentially.

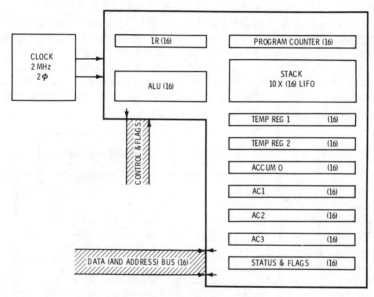

Fig. 3-26. PACE 16-bit CPU.

An indexed load instruction on PACE takes only 4 microseconds, with a 2-microsecond clock. This is 20 percent faster than the same instruction on the 6800.

Internally, the PACE is built like a 16-cylinder Mercedes-Benz, with four 16-bit accumulators, a ten-word "last-in, first-out" (LIFO) stack, two temporary scratchpad registers, and a 16-bit ALU.

Because many microcomputer applications chiefly involve the control of some complex assembly process, or chemical cycling, or mechanical flow control, PACE was designed to be a Processing And Control Element (hence the name PACE). This was accomplished by including a rather sophisticated six-level vectored priority interrupt right on the chip. The hardware can save all the internal registers in the ten-word LIFO stack, along with the vector of the interrupt. No software polling is required, as in many of the 8-bit machines. With this type of interrupt system, the PACE can be used as the master controller of a complex real-time process cycle involving many external devices and sensors.

SC/MP—The SC/MP (Fig. 3-27) processor (pronounced "scamp") offered the first really cost-effective microprocessor that could be used in low-cost controller types of operations, particularly ones involving mechanical operations or serial data. The best thing about the SC/MP is its price, which is significantly lower than the fancier 6800s and 8080s.

With regard to hardware, the SC/MP is among the simplest of processors to use, hosting three 16-bit pointer (index) registers, a flexible 8-bit ALU, and an "extension" register that can be used either as an internally programmed register or as a serial input or output port. The SC/MP can easily send serial data right off the chip into a receiving device, and vice versa.

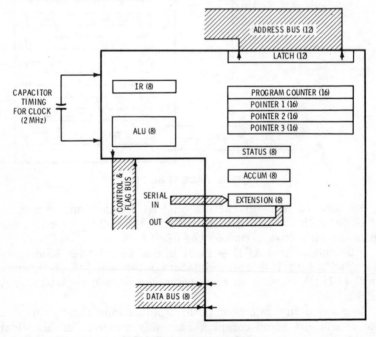

Fig. 3-27. SC/MP 8-bit CPU.

Moreover, the SC/MP has three external flag pins that can be set or reset under program control.

The IC has two sense inputs, one of which serves as an interrupt pin to allow a single vectored interrupt. Software polling must be used to determine the interrupting device when more than one device is to be serviced. Twelve full bits of address come right off the pins. The remaining 4 bits are available by latching them off the data bus at the proper strobe time. The data word is available on an 8-bit Tri-State bidirectional bus, and, just as in the more expensive machines, control of the bus is possible for DMA-type applications.

The SC/MP hardware arrangement has the simple efficiency of the early Volkswagen. The chip needs no clock and uses a single capacitor to set the frequency of the clock. (For more stable applications, a crystal can be used.) The most outstanding feature of the chip, however, is the bus request and bus grant process used in the SC/MP. The SC/MP is designed so that it can work in series with other SC/MPs. This type of multiprocessor operation is called *distributed processing*. By simply hooking the chips together in a daisy chain, a priority type of processing is put into action, with each SC/MP working on an individual part of the operation. A bus request pin on the processors allows them to share a common bus.

All the processors covered so far have been single-chip designs. Another class of microcomputers is the board-level systems, such as the LSI-11. The LSI-11 is a four-piece chip set on a single pc board. Its processing power and software support make it a device worth knowing about.

LSI-11—The LSI-11 microprocessor is an LSI chip set that emulates exactly the entire instruction set of Digital Equipment Corp.'s PDP-11 computer products. These devices have been in use since 1970, and have acquired an extensive software library, as well as a significant amount of applications experience.

The microprocessor is built around four n-channel MOS chips, which include a control and data element, and two microcoded (microprogrammed) ROMs. These ROMs are programmed to emulate the PDP-11 instruction set, and have a special routine for debugging on-line programs, operator interface, and bootstrap loading ability.

The LSI-11 is built on a single 8.5-inch by 10-inch circuit board. A second ROM allows hardware multiply and divide operation. Unlike most microprocessors that require some sort of control panel, the LSI-11 is designed to use a regular tty or crt/ASCII keyboard to communicate with the processor. The ROM chip contains all the necessary program code for these operations, along with code for controlling the CPU, examining internal registers, etc.

The address and data word length is 16 bits. The LSI-11 can directly access up to 64K bytes of 16-bit memory and can handle either words (16 bits) or bytes (8 bits) with equal ease. Stack processing in external memory is provided, along with a vectored interrupt input. A daisy-chained priority bus system is used, along with a bus grant output to allow multiprocessor operation. The LSI-11 system is designed to use a master/slave type of bus sharing. Each device using the bus can be a bus receiver or a bus transmitter, and only one device can send on the bus at any given time. This allows a very simple bus interface in the LSI-11, along with simple DMA capability.

As for software, the LSI-11 is the starship of the microprocessors. It contains a special power-fail-restart circuit that saves all important registers whenever the system senses dc power dropping. When power is re-established, the computer responds with the time that the dropout occurred and the status of the machine at this time. The LSI-11 software library covers almost every possible type of language, including FORTRAN, BASIC, and COBOL. Editors and assemblers are available, as are a large array of user application programs.

MEMORY

In its most basic form, computer memory can be represented as a single flip-flop storage unit. A flip-flop is a *two-state* device that can be made to store a single *binary* dig*it,* or *bit.* Since a bit can be either a 1 or a 0, the flip-flop will store either a 1 or a 0.

The flip-flop remains in either the 1 or 0 state as long as power is applied. At any time, the flip-flop storage unit may be read to determine what state it is in (Fig. 3-28). Also, at any time the state of the flip-flop may be set to a 1 or a 0 by applying the proper logic signal and pulsing the clock input. We call this operation a memory *write*. Determining the flip-flop's state is called a memory *read*.

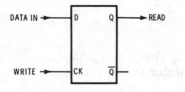

Fig. 3-28. A flip-flop is a 1-bit memory.

A word of binary information, such as an 8-bit byte, may be stored in a group of 8 flip-flops, as shown in Fig. 3-29A. If the inputs and outputs of the flip-flops are properly interconnected, the 8 binary digits can be made to enter and exit from the group in sequential or serial fashion (one bit at a time), or move in parallel—all 8 bits at once.

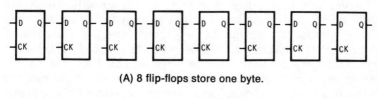

(A) 8 flip-flops store one byte.

(B) 8-bit register in the CPU.

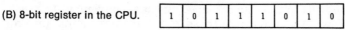

Fig. 3-29. An 8-bit memory.

When dealing with registers inside the CPU or memory, programmers usually draw them as shown in Fig. 3-29B. This simplified model of the storage cells makes it easy to illustrate register and memory locations.

Addressing

By simply increasing the number of these storage flip-flops, we can increase the number of storage words. But a fundamental problem presents itself: How do we locate a particular storage word or cell among a group of registers or memory locations?

The solution is to use a form of addressing. We can apply a unique group of binary digits to a group of pins, and a storage location becomes available. Fig. 3-30 shows how a typical semiconductor memory device is arranged so that the storage flip-flops, or "cells" as they are sometimes called, can be independently selected with a unique binary code called an *address word*.

Once the cell has been located, an input port on the IC is enabled, and a 1 or a 0 may be written into the cell. Inside the IC the cells are actually arranged in an x by y matrix, with half the address pins locating the x coordinate of the cells, and the other half of the pins locating the y coordinate. This is explained in detail in Appendix B, but for now it is sufficient to regard the cells as simply a long chain of flip-flops and the address as somehow moving a selector to the correct cell.

To read the state of a cell, the desired address is applied and the read line is enabled. Now the data in the selected cell appear at the output port. Note that the length in bits of the memory is equal to the number of storage flip-flops in the memory chip, and that the number of address pins is equal to n, where 2^n is the number of storage flip-flops. For example, a 256-bit memory chip is usually organized so that it has only one input and output port. Thus, it is called 256×1 memory. It has exactly eight address pins because $2^8 = 256$.

Larger microcomputer memories of 1K to 32K words are made up of many smaller ICs. The reason for using so many ICs is because of the number of interconnections necessary. At present the maximum chip density has reached 4K bits, but manufacturers are now striving towards 16K bits. For hobbyists or experimenters on a small budget, 1K-bit memories are the easiest to find and use. These are arranged as 1024×1, and come in 16-pin packages, making them convenient to use.

How do you arrange these $2^n \times 1$ memory chips into a suitable array on a printed-circuit board for use in a microcomputer system? For example, suppose you have a source of low-cost 1024×1 RAM memory chips, and you want to find out how many you need to make 4K words of memory for your 8-bit computer. Eight of the 1024×1 ICs arranged as in Fig. 3-31 produce 1024 words, or 1K words, of memory. For every input word, each IC stores one bit of the word (⅛ of the word). The address pins of the ICs are connected in parallel, and the

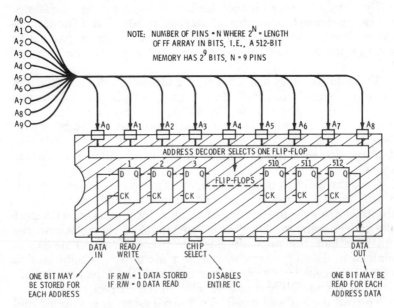

Fig. 3-30. A memory IC is an array of flip-flops.

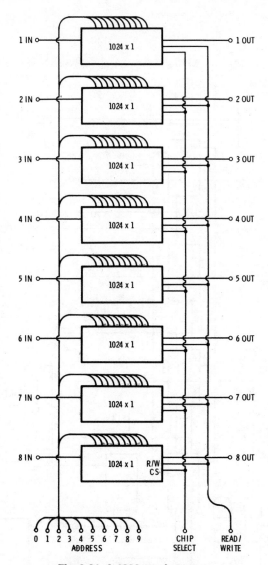

Fig. 3-31. A 1024-word memory.

8-bit binary data word is applied to the eight data-in pins. The output word is read off the eight data-out pins. Since eight ICs give 1K words of storage, it takes four of these circuits, or 32 ICs, to make a 4K-word memory. This is shown in Fig. 3-32.

The reader might have noticed that a 4K memory has 2^{12} words of storage and, therefore, requires a 12-bit address. However, our 1024×1 chips have only 10 address pins. The

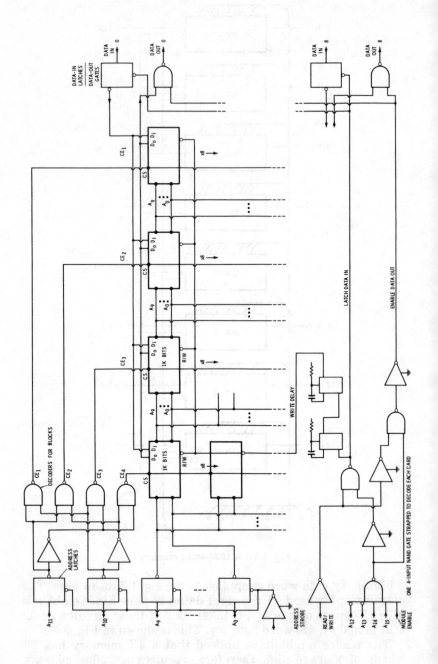

Fig. 3-32. A 4096-word memory, which uses 32 1K-bit ICs.

solution to this problem is to use the chip select (CS) pin of the ICs to enable a single block of 1024 words at a time. In effect, we decode the eleventh and twelfth bits of the address into one of four, which in turn selects the desired 1024-word block. Note that we show 16 bits of address in this circuit; bits 12, 13, 14, and 15 are used to select one particular 4K memory card, out of a total of 16 cards. These high-order address bits are decoded by a five-input NAND gate which is hard-wired to strap the card in at the proper address. These cards make up 4K-word pages in the total 64K word memory. There are 16 possible pages, since there are 4 more bits decoded in the address. Fig. 3-33 shows a complete 2048-word microcomputer memory, complete with transceivers for interfacing to a bidirectional data bus. Fig. 3-34 illustrates a commercial semiconductor memory board.

Speed

The 1024-bit 2102 memory chips we have discussed are fabricated by using the "n-channel MOS" manufacturing process. Economy versions of the 2102 have cycle times of under 1 microsecond, and premium versions are under 200 nanoseconds. (*Cycle time* of a memory chip is how long it takes from the time a valid address is applied to the chip, to the time valid data appear at the output of the chip.) Since the microcomputer usually performs most of its instructions by addressing memory, it is often memory read and write (and cycle) times that set the speed limit on certain programs. Some microcomputers will insert a wait command between a memory write or read instruction to slow the processor down to the speed of the memory ICs used.

The fastest memory circuits are ECL, or emitter-coupled logic. This type of logic cell works on current instead of voltage, and a 1 is so many microamperes and a 0 is so many less microamperes. Obviously, it is not a good choice for low-cost easy-to-use computer memory, as logic levels can be checked only with a sophisticated current probe, or by opening the connection physically and inserting a microammeter. Another problem with ECL is that it is so fast that triple-layer pc boards are a must. The middle layer of the board is a ground plane which helps to reduce the rf radiation caused when the ECL gates switch from one state to another. ECL also requires rather hefty power supplies.

Another popular fast memory chip is Schottky-clamped TTL logic. A Schottky diode is a special type of diode that has a metal in contact with the semiconductor device. This results in no charge storage at the junction, which normally prevents

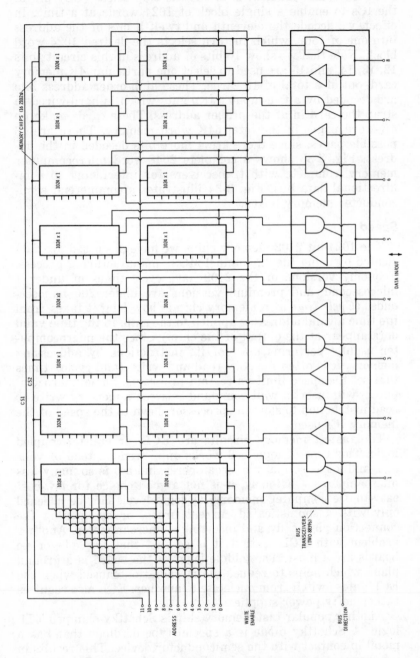

Fig. 3-33. A 2048-word memory with bus transceivers.

Courtesy Electronic Arrays, Inc.

Fig. 3-34. Photo of memory board.

transistors from switching above a theoretical maximum frequency. Schottky diodes are usually gold-dipped and are required on every TTL input. They are, therefore, an expensive form of memory. They are very useful whenever the need for high-speed TTL-compatible memory is needed.

Volatility

The perfect memory uses no power and stores data forever. Typical n-channel and p-channel MOS and TTL ICs dissipate around 250 to 500 milliwatts per chip. A 4096-word memory can easily draw 2 amperes at 5 volts. Obviously, this is far from ideal. If the power lines were to drop out for a few seconds, all the bits would change and the computer memory would end up with pure garbage in it. One approach to this problem is to take advantage of the chip select inputs on the ICs and force the chips into a low-power inoperative state when they are not involved in a memory read or write. Although the amount of power saved can be significant, the amount of additional circuitry may not warrant such a solution. Moreover, the processor must somehow go into a "power down" routine, which requires some special programming.

A more viable solution to this problem of losing stored information (volatility) is to use memory ICs made of CMOS. This logic family uses two MOS transistors instead of one, as in regular MOS, and draws almost zero power when not being read or written into. The CMOS transistor cells, however, are bigger than the regular MOS types and are thus more expen-

105

sive. They are perfect whenever low power consumption is required, such as for battery-operated microcomputers in remote locations.

Another approach to the volatility problem is to use dynamic memory. This type of memory cell uses a capacitor and a single MOS transistor to store a bit. The capacitor hangs on the gate of the MOS transistor, and must be refreshed every few milliseconds to keep it from losing its state. A few milliseconds in microcomputer time is almost an eternity, and with some additional circuits the refresh cycle can be squeezed-in between instructions. What the memory gives us in return is reduced power consumption, as there is one less transistor per memory cell. Dynamic memory can be hard to troubleshoot without a good dual-trace triggered scope, and should be avoided unless one can be sure of its reliability. (See Appendix B for more on the structure of the dynamic and static MOS cells.)

PROMs and ROMs

As we have seen, read/write memory has a volatility problem when designed around conventional semiconductor memory circuits. A more ideal memory would be able to store its contents indefinitely and never lose data. It would also have the same high access speed as semiconductors. The read-only memory, or ROM, serves exactly this purpose.

By setting up the desired bit pattern during the manufacturing process, the data in the memory may be permanently stored. In other words, the ROM memory is identical with a read/write memory except all the bits are fixed to a logic 1 or a logic 0. Thus, if the bit pattern in the ROM is fixed, there will be no data input pins, and the device will only be able to supply data, i.e., read only. As we will see, however, it is possible to write into a ROM if we loosen up on the definitions of writing. Keep in mind that only the small RAMs have separate data-in and data-out pins. Larger memory chips combine these pins as described under bus systems, and use a read/write control pin to determine the function of the pins. This allows the remaining pins to be used as address pins. A read/write pin won't be found on the ROM, but there will be a chip enable pin that takes the ROM from an inoperative state to the working state.

The usual way to use a ROM is to design and debug a program in standard read/write memory until it is working correctly. A listing of the bit pattern for the program is then sent to the ROM manufacturer. The manufacturer makes up a special mask and produces the ROM memory. The user receives the ROM and places it in the computer where the RAM memory was. If no mistakes were made, the program will perform exactly as it did when it resided in RAM. Note, however, that there is no way to correct a mistake in the ROM without starting all over, and that may take months.

A way around the long developmental cycle is to use what is known as programmable read-only memory, or PROM. Although the name may seem like a contradiction in terms, PROMs do exactly what their name says; they are read-only memories that may be programmed or altered. Here, programmed means that they are easier to alter than the "mask" ROM.

For example, the most basic form of PROM is made up of diodes. As shown in Fig. 3-35A, a diode can be made to act as either a logic 1 or a logic 0. If the diode is placed at the cross junction of an address bus to which several diodes are connected in common, the group will work as a complete word of stored data, as shown in Fig. 3-35B. The diode PROM is programmable in that the diodes may be removed with a soldering iron without damaging the memory.

There are several drawbacks to diode PROM (DPROM?). One is its large size when compared with IC memories. Another is its high cost per bit. However, for very short utility programs not exceeding, say, 32 bits (four 8-bit words), diode PROM may work fine. A third drawback to diode PROMs is

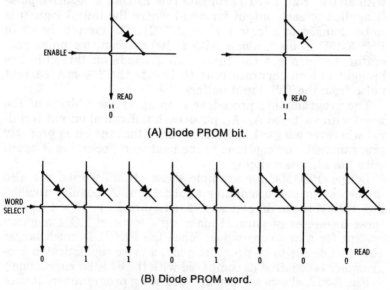

(A) Diode PROM bit.

(B) Diode PROM word.

Fig. 3-35. Functioning of diode PROM.

that the address rows and columns must be decoded with transistors or ICs to select the proper diode in the matrix.

More useful are the PROMs available with the same packaging as regular RAMs. These PROMs are programmed "electrically" by using a commercial programmer device or a homemade version. There are two types of PROMs now in popular use: fusible-link and erasable programmable.

Fusible-Link PROM—This type of PROM is like a regular memory IC, but instead of containing flip-flop storage cells, it contains tiny Nichrome fuses at each cell location. The fuse is connected in the PROM cell so that while it is intact, it will cause the cell output to be a logic 0. When it is electrically blown by the programming device, the cell output becomes a permanent logic 1.

Fig. 3-36A shows a popular 64-word fusible-link PROM that can be programmed quite simply. Each input to the PROM is a TTL load, while each output is an open-collector transistor. Fig. 3-36B shows that each bit of the data word is connected to one of 64 word-select columns, depending on which word is addressed. A fuse exists between the data pin and the emitter of a transistor. If the transistor is enabled by addressing the desired word *and* the fuse is intact, the bit will be read as a logic 0. But, if the fuse is blown out, the bit will be raised high and the pin will be at logic 1.

When you buy a new PROM, it may come preprogrammed with all 0's or all 1's. To program this PROM, a negative pulse is applied to each output terminal where the initial logic 0 is to be changed to a logic 1 (Fig. 3-36C). The circuit shown in Fig. 3-36D is used, along with a 100-milliampere pulse generator, to burn out the fuse. Two grounds on this chip are brought out on separate pins to isolate the 100-mA current pulse from the TTL input buffers.

The programming procedure is to apply the address of the word with switches A_0–A_5, pulse each individual output terminal wherever a logic 1 is desired, verify that the bit is properly programmed, and continue to the next word, selecting it again with the address switches.

Larger PROMs, for example those of 256 words, are also important in microcomputer applications. A popular fusible-link PROM is the Signetics 8226. Organized as 256×4, two of these memories in parallel make up a low-cost ROM memory system for a microcomputer. Since the PROM is much larger now (1024 cells to be programmed), a more sophisticated programmer is required as compared with the 64×8 programmer.

Fig. 3-37A shows a schematic of such a programmer. It uses toggle switches to select the desired address and momentary

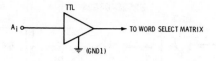

(A) Input circuit (×6).

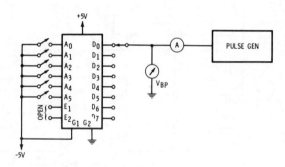

(B) Output circuit (×8).

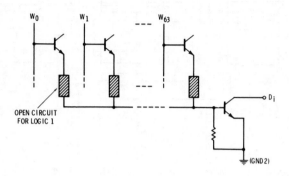

(C) Programming connections.

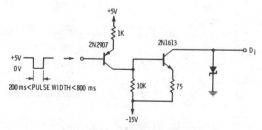

(D) Programming circuit.

Fig. 3-36. Fusible-link PROM (Harris 64 × 8 "HPROM").

82S26-82S29

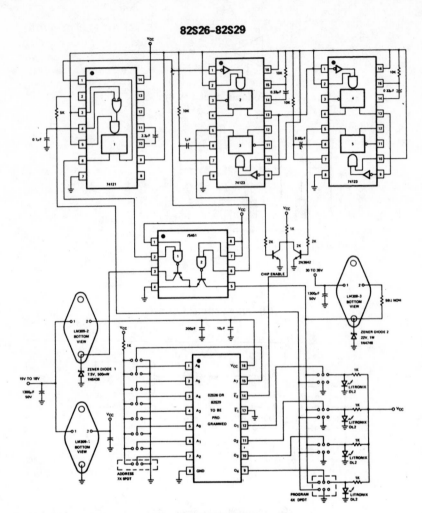

(A) Programmer.

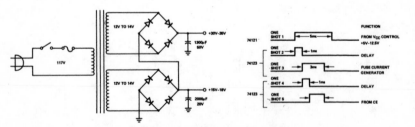

(B) Power supply and waveforms.

Courtesy Signetics Corp.

Fig. 3-37. Fusible-link PROM programmer.

push buttons to program the desired bits. As in the previous fusible-link PROM, the output pin of the IC is pulsed with current to blow the fuse. In this circuit, a complete generator is shown. Also, in this type of PROM the programming voltages must be applied in a special sequence, as the timing diagram of Fig. 3-37B shows.

The procedure for using the programmer is to insert the PROM and set up the address of the location to be programmed, using the toggle switches. When any of the output push buttons on the data-out pins are pushed, a sequence of timing pulses triggers the various LM309 current and voltage regulators. After a 1-ms delay, an 85-mA, 22-volt constant-current pulse is enabled for blowing the Nichrome fuse in the chip. When the switch is released, the LED will indicate a logic 1, if it is on. If it is off, it means the bit fuse is still intact and the procedure must be repeated. After the bit is verified, the next bit is programmed, and finally a new word is addressed and the procedure repeated.

The fusible-link PROMs have the same drawback when it comes to correcting mistakes as do the masked PROMs. If the engineer makes a mistake, the entire PROM must be replaced. This simply means PROM programs should be kept short enough so that making a mistake doesn't mean losing many hours of work. Thus, the small 64 × 8 PROMs are preferred to the larger PROMs when used with a simple ROM programmer, since nothing major is lost if a mistake is made. Moreover, if the programmer is controlled by a microcomputer, then the actual programming cycle can be vastly speeded up.

Erasable PROMs—The erasable PROM, sometimes called EPROM, UVROM, or EAPROM, can store data indefinitely like the fusible-link PROM but can also be erased at any time and reprogrammed.

An EPROM storage cell is made of a single p-channel MOS transistor, with the gate lead floating and insulated from the rest of the circuit. A voltage in excess of 30 volts will cause electrons to avalanche through the insulator and build up a negative charge on the gate. The negative charge causes a conductive inversion layer in the channel connecting the drain and source. Since the surrounding insulating material has a high resistance, the charge will not decay for many years (see graph in Appendix B). The charged gate thus forms an "on" transistor, and therefore can be programmed as a 1 or a 0. Since the gate lead is not electrically accessible, the charge cannot be removed by an electric pulse. However, illumination with high-frequency ultraviolet (UV) light on the cell surface will cause a photoelectric current to flow, which will eventually remove all the charge, returning the cell to its initial condition. By placing a quartz window over the monolithic circuit that makes up the EPROM, the entire memory array is erased by a sufficiently long bath of UV light (2 to 10 minutes). See Appendix B for more details.

The programming requirements for the early versions of the erasable programmable memory were quite demanding as far as timing and power dissipation during programming were concerned. The first, and probably the most popular, EPROM is the 1702A. This device requires applying the programming pulses to three separate pins and complementing the address and data signals just before these pulses are applied. All the voltages to the EPROM must be of exact amplitude and duration, and may not be applied for too long, or the chip will burn out. Since the 1702A and similar-type EPROMs are organized as 256 or 512 8-bit words, hand programming can be agonizing, especially when the program gets above a couple hundred bits. Fig. 3-38 shows an EPROM programmer with ultraviolet compartment.

A more reliable and time-saving way to program these EPROMs is to use the microcomputer to do the job. For exam-

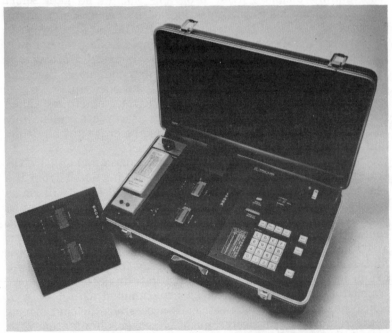

Courtesy Pro-Log Corp.

Fig. 3-38. Commercial EPROM programmer.

ple, a program can be developed in RAM where it is easily modified and debugged. Once the program is working properly, the microcomputer can use another program to copy, or move, the contents of the RAM into the EPROM, pulsing the EPROM pins with high voltage and programming the EPROM as it does so. As each programming cycle is finished, the microcomputer checks to see if the bits have programmed properly.

Notice that one subtle problem arises in using a program to manipulate and move another program. In this case the *copy* program must be written before it can do any copying! Since the most logical place to keep a copy program so that it won't be lost during a power outage would be in a ROM, this would mean we would have to hand program the copy program into the EPROM the first time around. If a mistake is made, we must start all over. The solution to this seemingly circular problem is to hand assemble the copy program the first time around in RAM. Then, after it is debugged and working correctly, have it copy itself into the EPROM! Now the copy program is safely stored away in a ROM, and can be called by a program as a subroutine at any time, to copy another program into EPROM. We can call the copy a "utility" program, and it can be kept in an EPROM called the "utility" ROM.

Other Uses for EPROMs—Permanent storage of microcomputer programs is not the only use of PROMs. We can further classify PROM as a dedicated component. A dedicated PROM can be programmed to be almost any kind of circuit. This is a consequence of the mathematical similarity between gates and bits. It is possible to take any type of digital gate and write its truth table on paper. So, since a PROM is nothing more than a giant truth table, we can make it work as any gate we wish, as long as we don't run out of bits in the PROM.

In Fig. 3-39A, an exclusive-OR gate and its truth table are shown. The XOR function can be stored in a PROM by simply using two of the input pins and one output pin, as shown in Fig. 3-39B. In this case we are programming the gate function in a low-cost, 64 × 8, fusible-link PROM. Since there are still four input pins left, two more XOR gates can be stored. Notice, however, there are five leftover output pins. These are actually wasted unless we make the inputs also represent other gate functions. (Such a program is described in Chapter 4.)

When using PROMs as code converters or large gate circuits, we must constantly look for ways to reduce the required number of input and output pins. This will help us keep the size of the PROM to a minimum.

As the size of the PROM increases, we can do more and more with it. For example, Fig. 3-40A shows a digital comparator

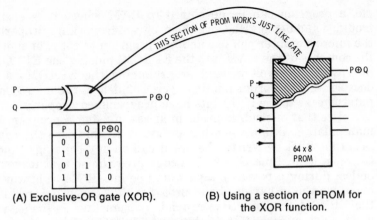

(A) Exclusive-OR gate (XOR).

(B) Using a section of PROM for the XOR function.

Fig. 3-39. Equivalency of gates and PROMs.

circuit made from a 256 × 4 PROM. It compares two 4-bit digital words on the eight input pins and produces the output signal corresponding to the relationship between the two words. If the words are equal, we get an output from O_1, A = B, and so on. The truth table for the PROM is shown in Fig. 3-40B.

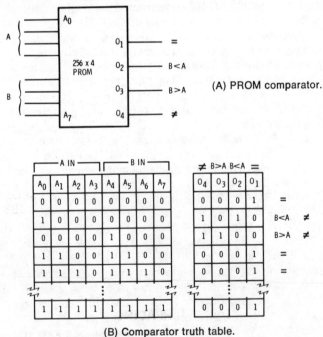

(A) PROM comparator.

A IN				B IN					≠ B>A B<A =				
A_0	A_1	A_2	A_3	A_4	A_5	A_6	A_7		O_4	O_3	O_2	O_1	
0	0	0	0	0	0	0	0		0	0	0	1	=
1	0	0	0	0	0	0	0		1	0	1	0	B<A ≠
0	0	0	0	1	0	0	0		1	1	0	0	B>A ≠
1	1	0	0	1	1	0	0		0	0	0	1	=
1	1	1	0	1	1	1	0		0	0	0	1	=
⋮													
1	1	1	1	1	1	1	1		0	0	0	1	

(B) Comparator truth table.

Fig. 3-40. PROM as a digital comparator.

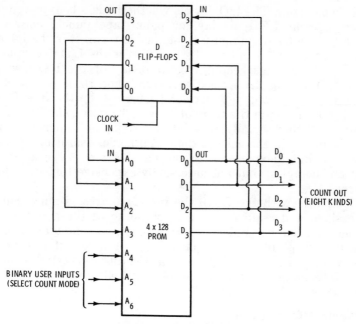

(A) PROM universal counter.

(B) Operating mode table.

USER BINARY INPUTS			
A_6	A_5	A_4	TYPE OF COUNT
0	0	0	BINARY UP
0	0	1	BINARY DOWN
0	1	0	BCD UP
0	1	1	BCD DOWN
1	0	0	GRAY
1	0	1	5-2-2-1
1	1	0	4-3-2-1
1	1	1	3-3-3-1

Fig. 3-41. PROM as a universal counter.

It's not unusual to see a PROM used as a programmable universal counter like the one in Fig. 3-41A. This is a 128×4 PROM, used in the feedback loop of a 4-bit synchronous counter. Four of the PROM's input pins are used to select the type of count, such as binary or bcd, and the direction of the count, either up or down. The operating mode table for this circuit is shown in Fig. 3-41B.

I/O INTERFACING

In the broadest sense, an interface allows us to put 1's and 0's into the computer. It also allows the computer to send 1's and 0's back out. The I/O device, whether it is a tv typewriter, seven-segment LED display, or paper-tape punch, converts these 1's and 0's to humanly recognizable form. It is the job of the interface to format the 1's and 0's for the I/O device and to control the housekeeping requirements of the I/O device. Most I/O devices are exceedingly dumb and therefore need a fair amount of control functions performed by the interface. The information, in the form of 1's and 0's, can come from the computer either serially (one bit at a time) or in parallel (all bits at once). In the case of the serial mode, operation is usually slow but inexpensive. In the parallel mode, operation is fast and complex (but not necessarily expensive for short distances).

Compared with the CPU, the interface area is much more diversified and requires an understanding of the many ways a computer can be "talked" to. In a sense, no computer is very useful (except for educational purposes) unless it has some minimum form of I/O. Let's look at the different types of possible interfaces, from a simple binary LED front panel to a complex ASCII keyboard.

Minimum I/O Interface

Perhaps the most basic form of interface is the one the machine-language programmer uses. In this case, the programmer at minimum will be able to enter data directly into the computer memory or examine the contents of a particular memory location.

LEDs and Binary Switches—To specify the memory address we will need a set of address switches, and to set up the data we need a second set of switches. The most basic form of front panel control will then consist of a group of toggle switches: 16 for address and eight more for an 8-bit data bus, giving a total of 24 switches. The data bus portion of a schematic for such a panel is shown in Fig. 3-42. The programmer communicates with the panel in 1's and 0's. This can be simplified by grouping the switches by threes or fours and converting mentally to octal or hexadecimal.

If the bus is Tri-State, we must be able to electrically isolate the switches from the bus. A set of 8833 bus transceivers can easily take care of this, and a momentary "push to write" switch will cause the data to appear on the bus.

Since we will want to be able to examine any area of memory, we will need some form of output display device. Eight LEDs driven by a set of 7475 latches can be used for this purpose. The latches hang on the respective address and data busses, and can be buffered for Tri-State operation with the receiver portion of the 8833 bus transceiver, as shown in the upper half of Fig. 3-42.

With this circuit the programmer can enter binary data through toggle switches, as well as examine data using the LEDs. The same sort of circuit will be required for the address bus if we want to be able to directly address memory. If the bus is 16 bits wide, we will need four 8833s and four 7475s. The same sort of LED/toggle-switch circuit is used. Finally, the programmer may want to have the program itself send data to the front panel. The simplest way to do this is to give the front panel a valid input/output address on the bus. In

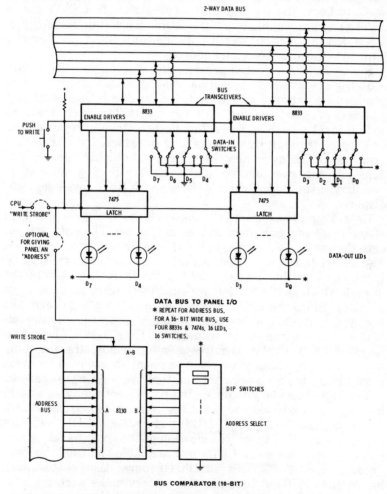

Fig. 3-42. Simple front-panel interface using toggle switches and LEDs.

other words, if we hard-wire an address comparator circuit to give an output for one and only one address, we can use this signal to latch the data on the bus from the CPU, and the program can access the front panel like a memory location. Such a bus comparator circuit is shown in lower Fig. 3-42. To allow flexibility, we can "strap in" the address with tiny DIP switches, which are switched occasionally with a pen or toothpick.

Since the front panel is now a valid memory location, we can write simple programs that do things inside the CPU, and then we can write the results into the front panel display for our analysis. For example, suppose the computer is stopped and we want to know the value of the accumulator. In such a case a short program would reside in a ROM, consisting primarily of a STORE instruction, which puts the contents of the accumulator into the specified panel address.

But as any experienced programmer can tell you, the binary switches are about as useful as sails on a battleship. It takes much more patience and time to set up the proper data and address information, and we must mentally convert machine code into 24 switch settings. Small "bootstrap" programs can be entered through this type of I/O interface, but if constant program reloading is necessary, this will quickly become burdensome. A better solution, and one not requiring much more circuitry, uses thumbwheel switches and LED seven-segment displays.

Octal Thumbwheels and Seven-Segment Displays—This type of interface is much more convenient to use. The data are put onto the bus by using three low-cost octal thumbwheel switches. These have four output lines per digit (coded in binary or bcd). If we choose either coding, and use the three least significant lines on the bus (2^0, 2^1, 2^2), we effectively form an octal digit (3 bits). Since the switches are connected inside to form the proper binary code, all we need to do is connect them to the bus transmitter portion of the transceiver (Fig. 3-43). The seven-segment LED display requires a latch to hold the incoming data, and three binary to seven-segment decoders to convert from binary to seven-segment and to drive the LED segments.

The logic necessary to define the panel electrically as a valid memory location uses the same bus comparator circuit shown in the previous binary LED I/O interface. Again, DIP switches can be used to "strap in" the location of the front panel.

Some seven-segment LEDs are available with all the 7447 decoders and 7475 latches built in. Of course, their cost is much higher than without these. However, they make wiring up the panel much simpler. But even thumbwheels become tiresome

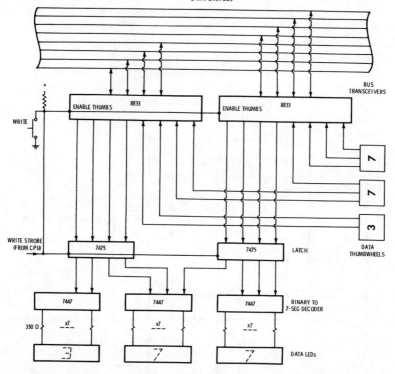

Fig. 3-43. Octal thumbwheel switches and seven-segment display interface. (Repeat for address bus.)

after awhile, especially if they are hard to turn. The obvious next step up in convenience is the old familiar calculatorlike keyboard.

Hex Keyboard, Maximum Hardware Circuit—The next level up from the octal thumbwheel display, and the one most often used by the manufacturers of low-cost microcomputer kits, is the hex keyboard and seven-segment display. The design of keyboard technique can be approached in one of two ways. One way involves an operating program that scans the keyboard matrix and determines which key is being pressed. The program then lights the appropriate LED digit. The second technique uses all hardware to generate and light up the digit. The second method is the most obvious; therefore we will cover it first.

Fig. 3-44 shows the details of the "all-hardware" keyboard system. The keyboard is made up of 16 single-pole switches (Fig. 3-44A). The switches are connected to a 16-input, 5-line–output, handmade diode PROM. The diodes are arranged so

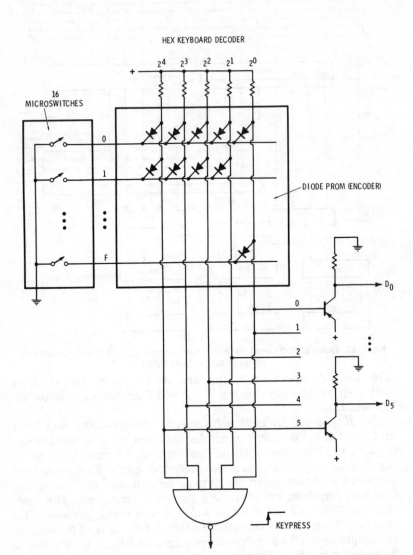

(A) Hex keyboard decoder.

Fig. 3-44. All-hardware

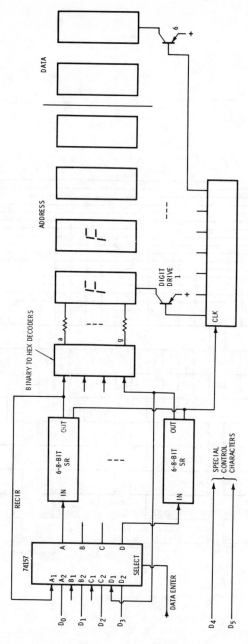

(B) Circulating digit approach.

keyboard system.

121

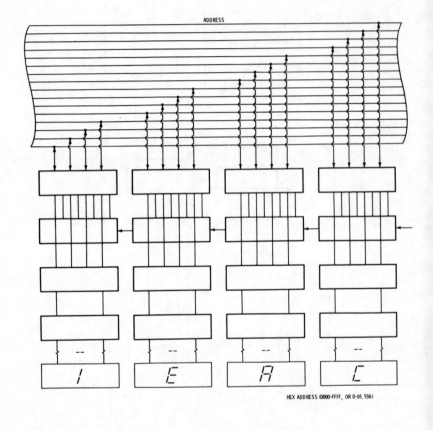

ADDRESS

HEX ADDRESS (0000-FFFF, OR 0-65, 536)

(C) Hex keyboard, bus interface,

Fig. 3-44. All-hardware

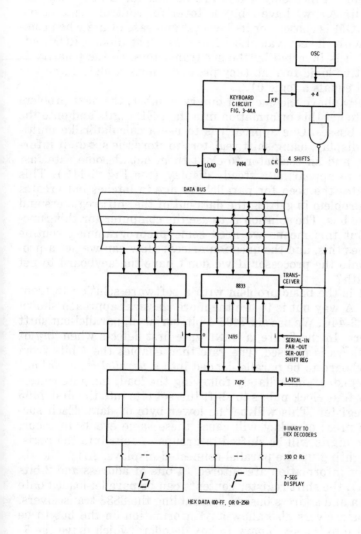

and seven-segment display.

keyboard system—*continued.*

that when one switch is closed, a 6-bit binary word appears on the output. We can arrange the PROM any way we wish, but for simplicity we make each key have the same value as its binary word. Since only 4 bits are needed for a hex code (see Appendix A), we have 2 bits leftover for control use later on. The PROM is chosen for its low cost and ease of use when compared with the equivalent TTL encoder. The diode PROM output word is inverted by the six transistors, so the polarity is in positive-logic format (key pressed equals a logic 1; no key pressed equals a logic 0).

Once we have the encoded binary number, the next problem is how to get this information into the LED digits and onto the proper busses. One approach is to use a calculatorlike multiplexed display, using shift registers to store the six-digit information, and an oscillator to clock them out at some rate fast enough to appear as a steady display (see Fig. 3-44B). This eliminates the need for parallel storage in latches but creates a new problem in getting the data out of the shift registers and onto the bus. The solution is to use the computer for this function. But this means we need some preprogrammed routine that does this, and the question arises: How can we get a program into the processor if we don't have the keyboard to get it in with?

That is the basic problem with a software solution to front panels. A way out is to use the more classical approach shown in Fig. 3-44C. We use six 7495 4-bit, serial-in, parallel-out shift registers. In the figure, a NAND gate first detects when *any* of the 16 keys is pressed. The gate then enables the 4 bits from the keyboard to be parallel-loaded into a *parallel in, serial out* shift register. Immediately following the load, the gate causes exactly four clock pulses to shift these 4 bits into the first 7495 shift register. This will be the lower byte of data. Each successive press of a key will cause these same events to occur, and the digits will be shifted in groups of four into the registers, lighting up the parallel-connected displays. After the six digits of information are entered (4 bits of address and 2 bits of data), the shift register contents can be parallel-loaded onto the data and address busses, by enabling the 8833 transceivers. The transceivers also allow any information on the bus to be latched into the six binary to hex decoders which drive the 7-segment displays.

Although the circuit requires more than 30 ICs, its conceptual simplicity and use of nonspecial parts make it a valuable and fast tool for debugging a microprocessor. The convenience of being able to simply press a button and have the number automatically decoded and properly placed on the bus is a good reason for using this approach. Furthermore, as we shall see, the other approach to keyboard interface requires an operating program.

Hex Keyboard, Software Approach—The software approach to a hex keyboard uses what is called a *scanning and table look-up* technique. The hardware shown in Fig. 3-45 contains a 5-by-8 matrix-type keyboard. In a scanning type of keyboard, an instruction sequence in the program applies the address of the keyboard to the five "rows" in the key matrix. The eight "columns" of the key matrix are pulled high by resistors, and form the inputs to two 8834 transceivers. The transceivers apply the information from the eight keyboard columns to the data bus. If no key is depressed, selecting and reading the keyboard will put all 0's into the accumulator. But if a key is pressed, a 1 will appear in the accumulator. Since the difference between a key press and no key press is a 1 in the accumulator, we can use a program that simply loops, checking to see when the accumulator becomes nonzero. When it does become nonzero, the program enters the next phase and determines which key was pressed. It does this by applying a row of the address and reading the corresponding data word. The row count is kept in a register, and when the data word finally becomes a number greater than zero, the number of the row containing the pressed key is contained in the register. The register value, along with the data word, is used to form the address in a table of the desired digital value for that key.

In order to minimize the decoders necessary for driving the LEDs, we can use the software to store the corresponding code for each of the 16 possible hex digits. After determining which key was pressed, we need to display its value in the LEDs. The CPU simply looks up the desired digit code stored in a table in memory and then applies this information to the seven segments, via the data bus. Since only one digit can be applied at any given time over the eight data lines, multiple digits are multiplexed by having the CPU scan the display while it also scans the keyboard. The software routine uses a pointer to store the number of digits in the display. Since the individual digits are stored in memory, the program selectively applies each digit to the display, via the data latches (74175), while enabling the respective digit via the address bus and the alternate two latches. The actual program that does this is quite interesting but takes some effort to decipher in a strange computer language.

The multiplexing requirement illustrates an interesting problem with software keyboards. Since the display is multiplexed, the program must constantly execute a loop to keep the

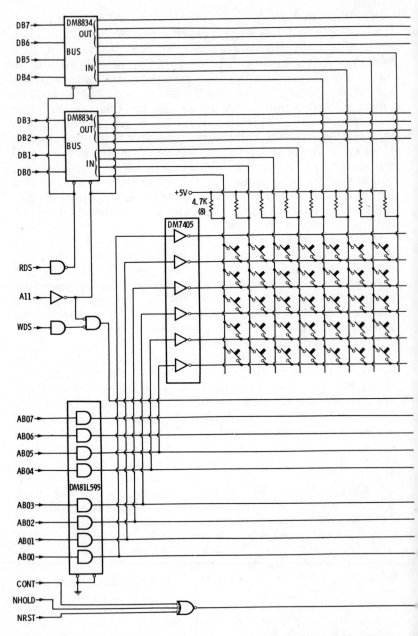

Fig. 3-45. Hex keyboard,

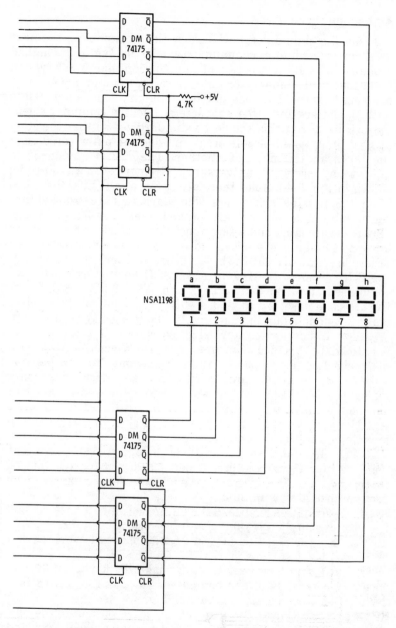

Courtesy National Semiconductor Corp.

software approach.

display visible. If the CPU breaks down or isn't working right, the panel operation will be rendered useless.

Alphanumeric Interface

From the simple hex keyboard with hex numbers, the next level up in computer communication is the familiar English alphabet with its numbers and punctuation marks. These can be encoded into binary for entry into the computer. Our first problem is to decide which particular binary codes to associate with the letters and other characters. Luckily, computer scientists realized that this should be standardized so that the storage medium would be universal and one computer could read the tapes and memory of another. The ASCII standard we know today meets this universal requirement with a 7-bit code, shown in Fig. 3-46. Since there are seven ASCII bits, there are 2^7, or 128, possible characters. The characters are grouped into seven subsets, as shown. All totalled, there are 32 words for uppercase alphabet and a few punctuation marks, 32 words for lowercase and a few marks, and finally 32 machine commands (these are transparent to the keyboard printer).

ASCII Keyboard—Having 128 ASCII characters means we could need up to 128 switch keys to make our keyboard. Luckily, the code is set up so that a shift command can be used to make keys double up in function. We have already seen how to decode a 16-key switch keyboard, so we ask if there is some way to adapt this idea. The answer is yes. We can, in fact, simply make four more sets of 16 keys and put them in parallel with the diode ROM. Now, when a key is pressed, it not only makes the 4-bit code but pulls one of four lines down. We can encode the one of four into 2 bits, giving us the fifth and sixth ASCII bit of our word. Finally, we add a shift bit to double the meaning of all the keys and pick up the seventh ASCII bit.

Rather than build your own diode ROM, however, you might want to investigate a complete keyboard encoder IC. One of these, the HD0165 for example, and some simple logic can be used to form a very minimum 48-character keyboard, as shown in Fig. 3-47. In this keyboard the lowercase alphabet is dropped for circuit simplicity. Since there is such a large market for keyboards, assembled 64-key "uncoded" matrix keyboards can be found on the surplus market for under $30.

The next thing we need to do is make the keyboard "interface" with the bus of the computer. Since the keyboard is a "sender" but won't always be sending, we need a set of bus drivers or transmitters to load the keyboard data onto the bus. We again use the approach of the hex-number keyboard and give the keyboard a valid memory address, using bus compara-

		000	001	010	011	100	101	110	111
	0000	NUL	DLE	SP	0	@	P	`	p
	0001	SOH	DC1	!	1	A	Q	a	q
	0010	STX	DC2	"	2	B	R	b	r
	0011	ETX	DC3	#	3	C	S	c	s
	0100	EOT	DC4	$	4	D	T	d	t
	0101	ENQ	NAK	%	5	E	U	e	u
	0110	ACK	SYN	&	6	F	V	f	v
RRRR$_2$	0111	BEL	ETB	'	7	G	W	g	w
	1000	BS	CAN	(	8	H	X	h	x
	1001	HT	EM	)	9	I	Y	i	y
	1010	LF	SUB	*	:	J	Z	j	z
	1011	VT	ESC	+	;	K	[	k	{
	1100	FF	FS	,	<	L	\	l	|
	1101	CR	GS	–	=	M	]	m	}
	1110	SO	RS	.	>	N	∧	n	~
	1111	SI	US	/	?	O	__	o	DEL

Control Characters

NUL	Null (All Zeros)	DC1	Device Control 1
SOH	Start of Heading	DC2	Device Control 2
STX	Start of Text	DC3	Device Control 3
ETX	End of Text	DC4	Device Control 4
EOT	End of Transmission	NAK	Negative Acknowledgement
ENQ	Enquiry	SYN	Synchronous/Idle
ACK	Acknowledgement	ETB	End of Transmitted Block
BEL	Bell, or Attention Signal	CAN	Cancel (Error in Data)
BS	Backspace	EM	End of Medium
HT	Horizontal Tabulation	SUB	Start of Special Sequence
LF	Line Feed	ESC	Escape
VT	Vertical Tabulation	FS	File Separator
FF	Form Feed	GS	Group Separator
CR	Carriage Return	RS	Record Separator
SO	Shift Out	US	Unit Separator
SI	Shift In	SP	Space
DLE	Data Link Escape	DEL	Delete

To find the character equivalent of a 7-bit binary number, divide the number into CCC RRRR$_2$ and look under the respective row RRRR and column CCC.

Fig. 3-46. ASCII standard computer code.

tor circuitry as discussed earlier. Now the CPU can address and read the keyboard.

Interrupt I/O Keyboard—How does the computer know when to check the keyboard device for a key press? This simple question is not trivial to answer. The two possibilities are: polling I/O, where the computer goes out and checks the device for a key press all the time (or at least quite often), thereby tying up valuable computer time; or interrupt I/O, where the keyboard interrupts the CPU from whatever it is processing, using the interrupt circuits found on the various processors. The decision between interrupt or polling is another tradeoff between software and hardware. For example,

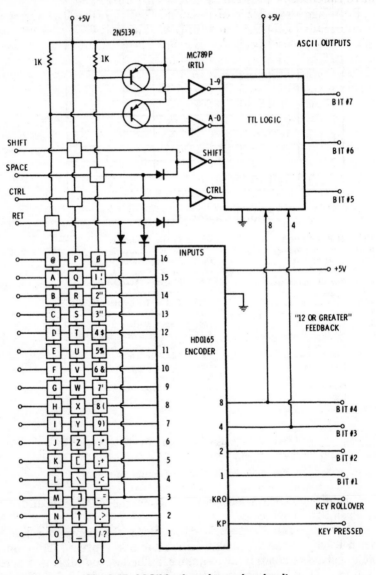

Fig. 3-47. ASCII keyboard encoder circuit.

it may be practical to write a fairly short program to get the character and put it in a memory location. The next time, it gets the character and puts it in the next location, and so on. Obviously, if you can write this program fairly fast and enter it manually into RAM or PROM (using a hex keyboard or binary switches), you have accomplished in software what may have taken days to build and debug in hardware.

But, the point of this digression is not to prove that one way is superior to another, but simply to illustrate the different side effects of the two methods. In a way, programming 1's and 0's is quite like wiring a circuit. Each wire you add causes the circuit to come closer and closer to the final schematic. In programming, each 1 and 0 you add takes you closer and closer to the final program flowchart.

Alpha Solid-State Display—So far, we have described the ASCII keyboard as a sender to the CPU, and said nothing about how we see what we are doing. This is the same problem we faced with the hex keyboard. Remember, then we used latches and seven-segment LEDs. It turns out that we can buy special LEDs that contain alphanumeric capability. Called *alpha solid-state displays*, these are made by using a 5-by-7 dot matrix of LEDs per digit, and require a special decoding circuit to function. The big question becomes: How many characters should we display? In other words, should we be able to see a single sentence of text, a single word, or a single letter? In essence, the width of the display is like a window into characters stored in the machine: the larger it is, the more we can see at once, and the easier the job of figuring out what is going on. But also, the larger the display, the more it costs.

On a more practical level, there is a display that allows us to present many lines of English text and doesn't cost a fortune. It is probably within 100 yards of where you are standing right now—the common television set.

Video Display Module—The video display module (vdm) takes us up quite a step in storage capacity from the alpha solid-state readouts. The vdm is used with a tv or video monitor to generate lines of text just as they are read on a printed page (Fig. 3-48). A typical vdm produces 16 to 20 lines of text, and each line has 40 to 64 characters. Since a typical word is five characters long (six, counting the spaces), we can get about eleven words per line with a 64 character/line vdm.

```
123456789012345678901234567890123456789012345678901234567890901234
         10        20        30        40        50        60
```

The above sequence of characters (numbers) gives us a relative idea of the kind of information density this represents.

Since there are 16 of these lines, we can expect 11 times 16, or about 200 words on the display at any given time.

The vdm in Fig. 3-48 has a 1000-word RAM buffer memory for storing characters. The computer only has to fill the buffer and tell the vdm where the text is to start. The circuit puts the characters on the screen in the proper sequence without interrupting the computer. The output is an EIA (Electronic Indus-

Fig. 3-48. Video display module.

trial Association) composite video 1-V_{pp} signal, with a bandwidth of 6.7 MHz. Such a wide bandwidth is directly due to the high storage density (64 characters are a lot of resolution). Usually the video must then go into a video monitor, rather than a standard tv, since the tv's i-f amplifiers may not be able to handle the wide bandwidth (most tv's have a 4.5-MHz bandwidth). The vdm is built around a *character generator* ROM with a character font like the one in Fig. 3-49. The IC accepts a 6-bit ASCII input, decodes it, and outputs 35 "dots" of 5-by-7 matrix information that describes the character on the tv screen. This, of course, gives only a single character. To store many characters, six 64-bit shift registers are used to circulate the ASCII data bits to the character generator ROM, which sends out the proper dot pattern to the tv. The six 64-bit shift registers each hold 64 characters, or a *line* of text. Additional storage is used to hold the remaining 15 lines, and usually this will be 2102 type RAM. The RAM itself may hold up

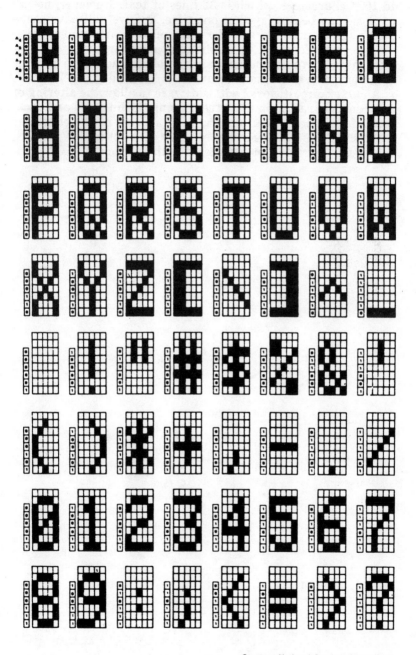

Fig. 3-49. ASCII character font.

to 1024 characters, which is 32 lines of text. However, not all of these can be displayed at one time, and we will have a *display* page of text and a *buffer* page of text. We read the display page while we fill up the buffer page. Various circuits inside the vdm route the special control characters to provide functions such as carriage return (CR), line feed (LF), etc.

A *cursor* circuit works with software to allow the altering of a random character on the screen. Using the line feed and backspace functions, we can generate the address of the character we wish to change. The computer then goes out to this address, erases the character, or replaces it with another.

chapter 4

PROGRAMMING

The computer's power as a machine lies in the fact that it can be "programmed" to perform various functions at the will of the user. This is the most distinct difference between the computer and any other sophisticated machine that has been created by man. In this chapter, we will learn what is meant by the term "program," and how one goes about writing (or designing) a program. We will work through some examples of commonly required programming techniques, and will discuss in detail the steps involved in writing a program.

EXECUTION OF A PROGRAM

We will begin by defining just what a program is. A *program* is a sequence of steps (or instructions) that must be performed in order for a desired process to be completed. A non-computer example of this is the steps necessary for the refinement of crude oil into gasoline. Mathematical examples are plentiful, such as the formula for determining the area of a circle: $A = \pi r^2$. The sequence of steps necessary for the solution of this formula is as follows:

1. Obtain a value for the radius r.
2. Square the value for the radius (or multiply it times itself).
3. Obtain a value for the constant π.
4. Multiply the squared radius (r^2) by the value for π.
5. Deliver the above product as the area A.

Now there are several ways to go about performing these steps, and as long as the same solution is found, the technique is not important. We intend here to illustrate the procedural nature of this step-by-step approach to problem solving. For each given radius, we must begin with Step 1 and proceed through Step 5 in order to have completed the job. Likewise, a program, stored in the memory of a computer, is a sequence of steps that direct the computer in its processing.

Programs in Memory

As we have learned, the computer is capable of executing only one instruction at a time, and it therefore requires a memory of some sort in which to store the complete set of instructions that make up the program. The amount of memory that is necessary to store the program depends on several factors pertaining to the complexity of the program and the amount of memory necessary to store data used by the program.

Execution of this program consists of taking one instruction at a time from the memory and performing the operation that it specifies. The program counter register (PC) is used by the CPU to step the program through execution, one instruction at a time. The PC usually contains the memory address of the instruction currently being executed. It is automatically incremented by the CPU just before the next instruction is fetched from the memory. The increment is added to the PC arithmetically, and its value reflects the size in words of the particular instruction that has just been executed. This increment varies between different CPUs, but the principle is the same. The normal sequence of executing instructions is to begin at low memory addresses and to proceed by adding positive increments to the PC, in order to step through the program which is arranged in ascending sequence in the memory.

Data in Memory

Various elements of data that are to be used by the program may also be stored in the memory. These may include such things as the value of π, used in the previous example. In order for the program to be able to use this numerical value, the memory location at which it is stored must be known by the program at the time that the value is needed. Another example of data in memory concerns the connection of some I/O device to the computer. Generally speaking, data that have been put in the computer are stored in the memory for future use by the program. In the case of complex I/O devices, where many words of data are being transferred at a fast rate, large blocks of memory may be reserved for storing these large amounts of data. Here again, the program must know exactly where this block is located in the memory and how large it is. The programmer must build these *data addresses* into the program, and he must make certain that all references to the data are consistent with these addresses.

Memory Map

Throughout this chapter, we will develop a program that performs a relatively simple task. That task is to move data stored in one area of memory into another area of memory. This is a very useful operation and is often required as a part of some greater processing goal. Fig. 4-1 shows a simple "map" of how the memory is to be allocated for this program.

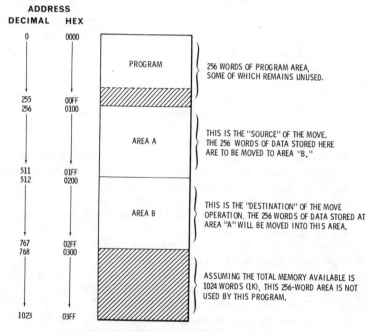

Fig. 4-1. Memory map for MOVE program.

For the purpose of illustration, we will be writing this program to operate on the Motorola MC6800 microprocessor, equipped with 1024 words (1K) of RAM memory. Keeping the development as simple as possible, without too many "bells and whistles," we should be able to get this program into 256 words of the memory. Using hardware, we will arrange it so that when the 6800 is reset, all registers including the program counter are set to zero; thus, the first executable instruction of the program must reside in memory location 1. The PC will be incremented just prior to fetching the instruction so that it points to the first word of the program. Although it is doubtful that we will use 256 words of memory for this program, we will allow some space in memory for expansion if desired.

There are two data areas, each 256 words in length. Our program will move data from area A into area B, one word at a time. Area A begins at memory location 256 (which is actually the 257th word of memory since the addresses start at 0) and extends through location 511. Area B begins at memory location 512 and extends through location 767. Memory locations 768 through 1023 are not used for any purpose by this program.

INSTRUCTION SET

The group of different instructions that a particular CPU is designed to execute is called its *instruction set*. Each manufacturer incorporates a slightly different instruction set into the CPU, according to the intended use of the product. Some are very simple, consisting of only a handful of instructions, while others are quite complex, with the total number of possible instructions ranging to several hundred. There are several different types of instructions, each having its own usefulness. The instructions are given names which are usually abbreviated in the form of some group of characters. Of course, inside the computer, these instructions are stored as binary 1's and 0's. An 8-bit instruction for adding two numbers might be 00101101. This is great for the computer, but it is a bit hard for programmers to remember, so the abbreviation *ADD* might be used in place of the binary code. These abbreviations of the instruction set are known as *mnemonics,* or the *operation codes,* of the instructions.

Just telling the computer to "ADD" is not quite enough. The computer must be told what to ADD, and what this is to be added to. This information is also considered as part of the instruction, and in fact is usually contained in another word (or words) of memory just following the actual operation code part of the instruction. There are exceptions to this as we shall see in the section on addressing modes, but, for the most part, each instruction must have a specified *operand*. This is the "who" that the "what" is to be done to.

Memory Access Instructions

In any instruction set, there are usually several instructions dealing with the operation of putting data into, or getting data out of, the memory. On the other end of this data transfer is usually some CPU register, most likely the accumulator, since this is where most of the "computing" is done. (See Fig. 4-2.) This operation can pertain to only one word of the memory at any given time, and therefore the operand part of the instruction will specify the address of the memory location that is to be affected by the instruction.

Memory access instructions include "LOAD" instructions, which are used to transfer data from the memory to some internal register. In some cases, when there is more than one register that can be loaded in this way, there will be different instructions for each register, with different binary bit patterns to designate the desired register.

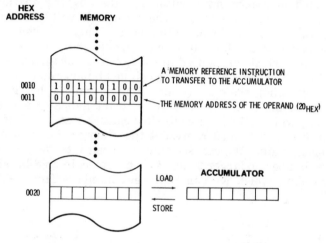

Fig. 4-2. Diagram of memory access instruction.

"STORE" instructions transfer data from some register in the CPU to a specific memory location. Again, where there are different registers that can be affected, the instruction will designate the desired register. The affected memory location can be designated in a number of ways (addressing modes) which will be discussed later in this chapter.

Arithmetic Instructions

The arithmetic instructions allow the program to control the ALU, causing the ALU to perform various types of arithmetic operations upon data stored in the accumulator register and in the memory. These operations are usually restricted to addition (Fig. 4-3) and subtraction in various forms, and only in the more advanced microcomputers will there be instructions for multiplication and division. As we shall see, these operations must be "programmed" by using the available set of instructions. Subtraction is often referred to as a "complement and add" instruction, since binary subtraction is accomplished by complementing the number and then adding, as shown in Appendix A.

In the usual situation involving arithmetic instructions, two numbers are operated on. Some CPUs require that both of these be resident in an internal register before the operation can be performed. The result of the arithmetic will end up in one of the two registers, thereby destroying the original contents. Other CPUs require that only one of the two numbers be resident in an internal register. The other number may be contained in a memory location specified by the operand of the instruction. The result of the arithmetic will be contained in the register after the operation is complete, and the contents of the memory location will remain unchanged.

The numerical values used in the execution of these arithmetic instruction are represented as signed binary numbers. Generally speaking, the sign (+ or −) is designated by the most significant bit of the data word. A 0 bit indicates a positive number, while a 1 bit indicates a negative number. The next seven bits in the word represent the binary equivalent of the numerical value. We can see that in seven bits we can represent a number no larger than 127. Therefore, in an 8-bit signed binary data word, we can represent numbers from −128 to +127.

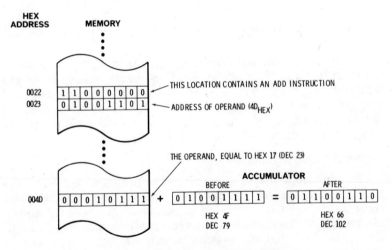

Fig. 4-3. Diagram of ADD instruction.

As positive and negative numbers are added and subtracted, the ALU automatically keeps track of the sign of the result. However, if the result of the arithmetic yields a number larger than +127, a processing error will occur, and the number will probably be mistaken by the computer for a negative number.

Logical and Shift Instructions

The ALU can also be controlled by the program to perform various types of "bit-manipulation" instructions. These are processed very similarly to the arithmetic instructions, in the sense that there must be data in an internal register, usually the accumulator. Shift instructions cause the contents of the accumulator to be shifted left or right in the register, bit by bit. This type of instruction does not access the memory at all but operates only on the contents of the accumulator. There are several good uses for this operation, one of which is that if we shift all the bits of a data word one bit to the left, we have in effect multiplied it by 2. (See Fig. 4-4.) Another use for this

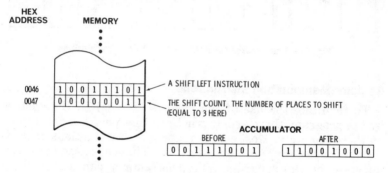

Fig. 4-4. Diagram of SHIFT LEFT instruction.

operation occurs when the program needs to determine which bits in a data word are 1's and which are 0's. If we start shifting the bits to the left, one at a time, every time a 1 bit ends up in the most significant bit of the accumulator, the word will look like a negative number. This condition can be used to tell the program whether the bit was a 1 or a 0.

The logical instructions provided by most microprocessors consist generally of the common logical operations AND, OR, and EOR. These require two operands, usually one in the accumulator and the other residing in some memory location. The standard approach here is that first one word of data is loaded into the accumulator and then the logical instruction is executed using the word from memory. The contents of the accumulator after the operation will contain the logical outcome, and the original contents will have been destroyed. The contents of the memory location are not altered by the logical operation. The truth tables for these instructions are shown in Fig. 4-5. The two data words are logically processed, one bit at a time.

These instructions are also useful in determining which bits of a given data word are 1's and which are 0's. For example, suppose we want to know if bit 4 of a word is set (equal to 1). We can load it into the accumulator and execute a logical AND instruction between it and a mask word that is set aside somewhere in memory and has bit 4 equal to 1 and all the other bits equal to 0's. If the desired bit is a 1, then the result in the accumulator will be the same as the mask word. If it is not a 1, the result in the accumulator will be all 0's.

AND TRUTH TABLE		
P	Q	PQ
1	1	1
1	0	0
0	1	0
0	0	0

OR TRUTH TABLE		
P	Q	P + Q
1	1	1
1	0	1
0	1	1
0	0	0

EOR TRUTH TABLE		
P	Q	P ⊕ Q
1	1	0
1	0	1
0	1	1
0	0	0

Fig. 4-5. Truth tables for AND, OR, and EOR instructions.

Register Manipulation Instructions

To facilitate the use of the various internal CPU registers by the program, there are instructions that perform operations on these registers. Most common are those instructions regarding the "index" or "pointer" registers. These are used for many purposes by the program. The programmer can assign them to be used for some general-purpose register, perhaps storing the address of some memory location that is accessed frequently. Some microprocessors dedicate one of these registers to contain the address of a special part of the program that is used to process an interrupt.

There are some instructions that allow the program to load a value into the desired register. These may be useful if there is something that needs to be done a fixed number of times by the program (such as read 80 characters from an input device). Here, the desired index register can be loaded with the value 80 and decremented (subtracted by one) each time a character is read. When the value in the index register is equal to zero, all 80 characters have been read.

Some instructions allow the program to store the contents of a given register in a location in memory. These offer the programmer the ability to save the contents of an index register while it is being used for some other temporary purpose, and then later restore it to its original value.

Certain microprocessors allow the program to access other registers besides the index registers, but they are exceptions. The National Semiconductor SC/MP has an "extension register," which is used similarly to the accumulator and is also used for the serial I/O port, as described in the section entitled "Input/Output Control."

There are some instructions that allow the program to exchange, or swap, two registers. This swap can be used to transfer the contents of the program counter to some index register for use at a later time. Since these are usually 16-bit registers in 8-bit processors, they generally must be manipulated in two parts, the most significant bits (MSBs) contained in one word and the least significant bits (LSBs) contained in another word.

Jump or Branch Instructions

Jump or branch instructions are capable of altering the program counter. This means that the program can "decide" which instruction to execute next, and need not always execute the very next instruction in the memory. The instruction may specify that a certain number of words be skipped over in the program and that execution be continued at some other address; or, an absolute memory address may be part of the JUMP instruction, telling the processor to jump to that address and resume execution.

These instructions give the programmer a great deal of flexibility in designing programs. If need be, the program can be made to jump ahead in the sequence of instructions, ignoring parts that do not pertain to a particular situation. The program can even be directed to jump back to some known point to repeat execution of instructions already executed.

In many cases, these jump or branch instructions must be accompanied by some necessary condition in order for the jump to occur. These conditions usually depend on the accumulator, which may be tested for several states, including positive, negative, odd, even, overflow, and carry conditions. The programmer may specify that the jump occur only if the result in the accumulator is a positive number, or perhaps the opposite. In this way, the program may be controlled by the results of various arithmetic operations involving the accumulator. This gives the programmer some real potential computing power, since what computers do best is impartially test for the existence of certain conditions and then invariably perform some desired process, based upon the test.

ADDRESSING MEMORY

Among the CPUs available today, the method used to address memory locations varies considerably in complexity. As we have seen, many of the instructions access the memory in order to store something there or to retrieve something previously stored. At the time that the instruction is being executed, the memory address of the location involved must be available to the CPU. This can be accomplished in many ways, depending on several factors, mainly the modes of addressing that are supported by the particular microprocessor in question. In this section, we will discuss some of the most popular forms of addressing memory.

Program-Counter Relative Addressing

This type of memory addressing allows the CPU to access words in memory that are located within a certain range of the

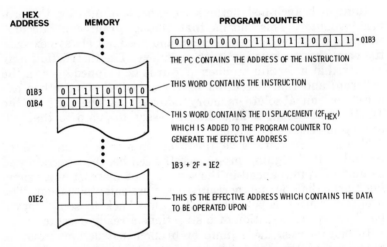

Fig. 4-6. Diagram of PC relative addressing.

current value in the program counter register. Since the PC contains the memory address of the instruction at execution time, the memory location being accessed by the instruction is within a certain range of the instruction itself. This range is generally limited by the word length of the microprocessor. The word directly following the instruction usually contains the displacement value which is added to the value in the PC to derive the effective address. (See Fig. 4-6.) This displacement can be positive, addressing memory locations with addresses larger than the address of the instruction, or it can be negative, addressing memory locations with addresses that are smaller than the instruction address. We can see that an 8-bit machine can accommodate displacement values of −128 to +127. This establishes the range about the PC value, within which the effective address must be.

The effective address is the address of the operand of the instruction. It is the contents of this address that are to be used during the execution of the instruction. This mode of addressing is useful for accessing memory locations that are close to the location of the instruction itself. Instructions using this mode of addressing will usually execute faster than other modes because only one memory access is necessary to load the displacement value into the CPU.

When the displacement is to be negative (that is, when the word to be addressed has an address that is smaller than the current value in the PC), the value of the displacement is stored in two's complement form. This data form is described in Appendix A, and the programmer should be familiar with its use, since many circumstances require a reference to a memory location with an address that is smaller than the address of the instruction currently being executed.

Pointer-Register Relative Addressing

Pointer-register relative addressing is very similar to PC relative addressing just described. The only exception is that a designated pointer register is used instead of the program counter to derive the effective address.

The displacement value is again stored in the word of memory directly following the word containing the instruction (Fig. 4-7). Its value can be either positive or negative, and it is added to the value stored in the designated pointer register at execution time to produce the effective address of the instruction. It is the contents of the memory location at the effective address that become the operand of the instruction.

This addressing mode is very useful in several ways. For one thing, the pointer register is usually a 16-bit register which can contain a value up to 65,535 in unsigned binary. This means that memory locations quite far away from the address of the instruction can be accessed. In fact, since the displacement value is still used in deriving the effective address, any memory location within the range of the displacement from the value in the pointer register can be accessed by the instruction.

Another benefit of this type of memory addressing is that the value in the pointer register can easily be modified by the program during execution. This means that the programmer need not know exact effective address at the time the program

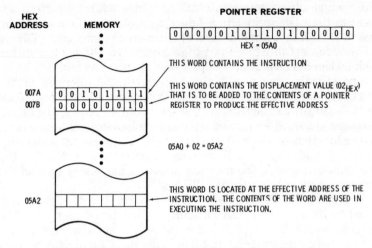

Fig. 4-7. Diagram of pointer-register relative addressing.

is written. However, the programmer must have some logical means for getting this information together at the time the instruction is to be executed, and for setting up the pointer register with the appropriate value.

Direct Addressing

In the direct addressing mode, the effective address is stored as an absolute binary number, usually occupying the two memory locations directly following the instruction itself. (See Fig. 4-8.) No program counter or pointer registers are involved.

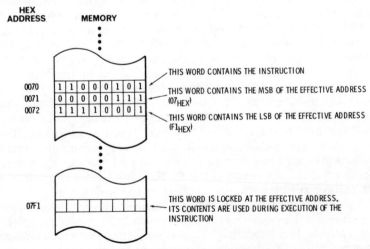

Fig. 4-8. Diagram of direct addressing.

The 8 most significant bits (MSBs) of the 16-bit effective address are stored in the word directly following the instruction, and the 8 least significant bits (LSBs) of the effective address are stored in the next word of memory. In some processors, such as the 8080, the order of these high and low address bytes are reversed.

This mode allows addressing any of 65,535 words of memory as the operand of the instruction. It is used mainly in situations where other modes are not sufficient. Memory locations can be accessed without regard for the limited range of a relative

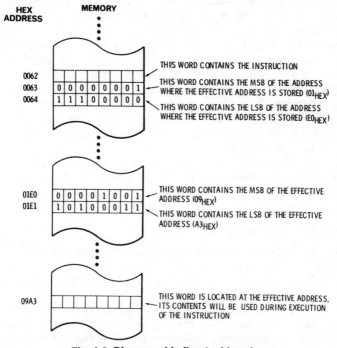

Fig. 4-9. Diagram of indirect addressing.

addressing mode, and also without requiring that a pointer register be set up and waiting. The only drawback to this mode of memory addressing is that it generally takes longer to execute, since two memory accesses are necessary just to acquire the effective address.

Indirect Addressing

The indirect addressing mode is one of the more sophisticated methods of generating the effective address. Not all of the microprocessors currently available offer this type of addressing. Its electronic support requirements are outside of the allowable cost effectiveness of some of the simpler CPUs, and it is mainly found in the more advanced general-purpose CPUs.

The unique feature of indirect addressing is that an intermediate step is involved. The operand of an instruction using this mode is an intermediate memory location that contains the actual effective address of the instruction. This intermediate address can be derived either by the PC or pointer-register relative displacement technique, or it can be defined "directly" as shown in Fig. 4-9. At this intermediate address is stored the effective address, usually occupying two memory locations: one for the MSB and the other for the LSB of the effective address. The CPU then proceeds to use this address and the data stored there during execution of the instruction.

The main advantage of this type of memory addressing is that the exact effective address of the instruction need not be known by the programmer at the time that the program is written. The address of the intermediate location is built into the instruction. Now, during execution of the program, the actual effective address may be determined by the program and placed in the intermediate memory location prior to the execution of the instruction.

The drawback here is, again, the fact that several memory accesses are necessary just to get the effective address into the CPU. These indirect instructions will take longer to execute than other types of memory addressing modes.

Immediate Addressing

Fig. 4-10 illustrates the immediate addressing mode. The operand address is also the effective address. The contents of the displacement word (which directly follows the instruction) are used as the operand for this type of instruction. No further memory accesses are necessary to complete execution of the instruction. Obviously, this type of addressing has many potential uses when a separate memory location for the data is not

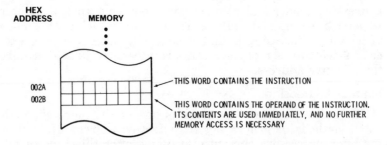

Fig. 4-10. Diagram of immediate addressing.

required. Because it requires no further memory accessing, this type of instruction usually has one of the fastest execution times.

Auto-Indexed Addressing

Auto-indexed addressing is basically the same as pointer-register addressing, but there is usually no displacement value in the word following the instruction. There is, however, one quite helpful variation on the pointer register principle. Whenever an instruction of this type is executed, the contents of the designated pointer register can be altered by some factor. The National Semiconductor SC/MP microprocessor is designed to use the value in the displacement word to alter the designated pointer register. If the value of the displacement is positive, it is added to the value in the pointer register after the memory fetch has been made. If the value of the displacement is negative, it is subtracted from the value in the pointer register before the memory fetch is made.

This feature is very useful when there are large areas of data stored sequentially in the memory that must all be operated upon by the program. (See Fig. 4-11.) A pointer register

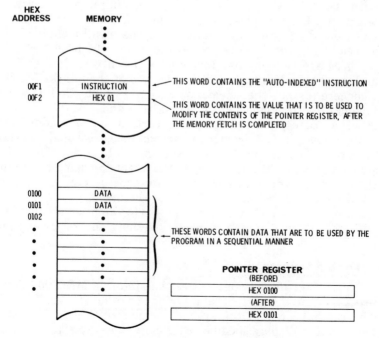

Fig. 4-11. Diagram of auto-indexed addressing.

can be set up to contain the memory address of the first word in the data area (lower memory address). The displacement word of the instruction that is to fetch these data words from the memory is set up to contain a binary 1. Each time this instruction is executed during the course of the program, the value in the pointer register will be incremented by 1 directly after the data are fetched. Thus, the next time the instruction is executed, the pointer register will contain the address of the next data word in the area.

Going one step further, the programmer should be aware that any value can be used as the increment if it is stored in the displacement word of the instruction. If this value were equal to 2 in the previous example, then every other data word in the area would be processed by the program as it was worked through.

INPUT/OUTPUT CONTROL

Input/output control refers to any situation in which the program has to execute instructions as part of a data transfer to or from a device. Most computer systems incorporate some sort of input/output device in order to interface the computer with the "real world." This may be as simple as a hex keyboard and LED display, or as complex as an ASCII keyboard and video display module. In any case, there will most likely be a need to control these devices at the will of the program.

There are two popular forms of I/O control: the *bus* type and the *instruction* type. Bus I/O is used as though the I/O device were just another memory location. In fact, the I/O interface is directly connected to the address and data busses, and is wired to respond to accesses of certain memory addresses. Instruction-type I/O control is accomplished through the use of special I/O instructions in the instruction set. These instructions access the I/O bus, which is not the same as any of the busses to which memory is connected. Input/output operations are conducted independently of the memory.

Both types of I/O control are useful to the programmer. We will look at an example of each, stressing the programming ramifications.

I/O on the Memory Bus

This I/O configuration utilizes the Motorola MC6800 microprocessor and the peripheral interface adapter (PIA). The I/O devices connected to the system include an ASCII keyboard and a video display module. Fig. 4-12 illustrates this input/output configuration.

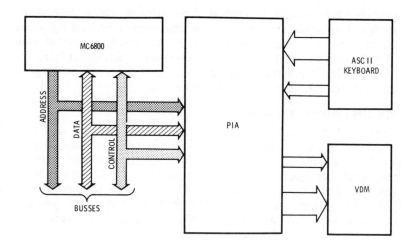

Fig. 4-12. I/O on the memory bus.

The PIA is an I/O interface that will control two devices. It is connected directly to the memory busses, at a special address. To operate the I/O devices, the program accesses this special address, and the PIA buffer becomes available to the program.

The input operation involves the receiving of characters from the ASCII keyboard. When a key is depressed, the PIA interrupts the processor and tells it that there is a character in the keyboard buffer. The program currently being executed must be put aside momentarily, and a JUMP instruction must be executed. The JUMP instruction goes to a series of instructions that will get the word containing the key-press information from the PIA buffer and put it into a CPU register. From there, it can be operated upon immediately, or it can be stored in a memory location until some later time. Once this has been done, the processor again resumes execution at the point in the original program where it was interrupted. This sequence of events occurs every time that a key is pressed, so the program instructions used to process this I/O operation must always be stored in the memory at some known location. These instructions are relatively simple for this example, since the PIA is treated just as if it were a memory location. When the character is ready to be read into the computer, the program simply executes a LOAD instruction, which transfers the contents of the PIA buffer into a CPU register.

The output operation involves transferring ASCII characters from the CPU to the video display module. We will assume that this vdm has its own internal memory in which the several hundred characters displayed on the screen are stored. The characters to be displayed on the screen are transferred, one at a time, to the PIA. This also can be accomplished with a simple STORE instruction, which addresses the special memory locations occupied by the PIA registers.

Special Instructions for I/O

This example of special instruction I/O uses the National Semiconductor SC/MP microprocessor. The I/O device is a Teletype keyboard and printer, in the conventional current loop with the Teletype control interface (Fig. 4-13). The actual entry into the CPU is done through the use of the special extension register inside the SC/MP. The MSB and LSB are connected directly to pins on the chip package. This register is controlled by special instructions in the program.

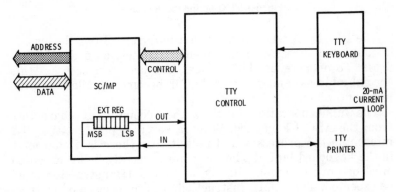

Fig. 4-13. Special I/O bus.

Bearing in mind that Teletype is a serial code, with the bits being transferred one at a time, notice in Fig. 4-13 that the Teletype control unit is connected to the serial I/O pins on the SC/MP. When a serial I/O instruction is executed, the logic level on the IN pin is transferred to the MSB of the extension register and the LSB of the same register is transferred to the OUT pin. All the other bits in the register are shifted one bit to the right.

The Teletype control unit must signal the processor when each of the data bits is present on the input pin. The program in midexecution is interrupted, and a jump is forced to the area of the program that is designed to process the I/O. The special serial I/O instruction is used to capture the bit and to shift it into the extension register in the CPU. After a certain number of bits have been read into the computer in this manner, the bit pattern in the extension register will be a representation of one character of input data.

For output operations, a character of the data to be output is loaded into the extension register. Then, through a time-delayed looping program, the serial I/O instruction is used to shift the bits out to the Teletype controller one at a time, at the correct rate of speed. The programmer would probably write the necessary instructions into a subroutine that could be used over and over to process the I/O. This subroutine could be incorporated in several programs for controlling the Teletype I/O.

A word about the Teletype controller. It is an interface that is in series with the 20-milliampere current loop, common to Teletype operation. The making and breaking of this current loop, which is used to encode each character, is converted to a changing voltage signal and applied to the IN pin. Likewise, the changing voltage on the OUT pin, which represents the data bits being transferred out, is converted to makes and breaks of the current loop. This causes the mechanical elements in the printer to select the proper character to print.

PROGRAMMING TECHNIQUES

Although the digital computer is a powerful problem-solving instrument, there are certain rules or principles that limit the capabilities of any digital computer. This fact is evident in the many similarities between the computer products of different manufacturers. These similarities are due not so much to the wish to standardize computer products, as they are to the limitations of the binary logic system.

For this reason, there are many instances where the programming method used to achieve some desired processing goal is precluded by the hardware features of the particular CPU. Such a simple operation as the addition of two numbers requires that the two numbers to be added first be identified (usually by memory addresses specifying the memory locations in which the numbers are stored). Next, one of the numbers must be loaded into a CPU register available to the ALU. The other number must also be made available to the ALU. This can be done with certain microprocessors by specifying its memory location address as the operand of the ADD instruction. Other processors require that both numbers be loaded into two separate CPU registers before the ADD can take place. Once the arithmetic has been accomplished, the result is usually present in some CPU register, and it may either be used in another arithmetic instruction directly following or be stored in a specified memory location for future use.

Other, more complex operations also will be found to follow certain procedural rules demanded by the binary processing approach. We will examine three of the most common programming techniques in terms of their procedural requirements, and not in consideration of any given manufacturer's product. The emphasis will be upon the step-by-step approach to achieve the processing goal, rather than on actual instructions for any particular CPU.

Iteration

Many times in the course of executing a program it becomes necessary to repeat a particular operation several times. This repeating process is known as *iteration*. It is a very common programming technique and can be implemented in a number of ways. The basic goal of iteration is to cause something to occur for a given number of times, or until some other condition is met. This technique can be used for counting events or for generating sequences of memory address for accessing large tables of information.

There are four general steps to the iteration process:

1. Initialize the counter. This initial condition is usually a word in memory or in a general-purpose register in the CPU. Either the counter can be initialized to zero and added to until some desired value is reached, or it can be initialized to the value and subtracted from until zero is reached.
2. Increment (or decrement) the counter each time that the process to be iterated is executed.
3. Test the counter each time the iterative process is completed, to see if it has reached the desired number.
4. Go back to the beginning of the iterative process if the desired number has not been reached.

Processing of this type is often called *looping*, since the same sequence of instructions is executed several times under the management of the counter. The program "loops" back to the beginning until the desired value is reached by the counter (Fig. 4-14).

The iteration process is useful when many elements of data are to be subjected to the same processing. These data may be read from some input device, one element at a time, or they may all be stored in the memory in sequential locations. Here, an internal CPU general-purpose register would probably be used for the counter. This could be initialized to the address

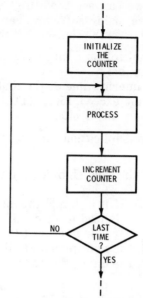

Fig. 4-14. Flowchart of the iteration process.

INITIALIZE THE COUNTER

PROCESS

INCREMENT COUNTER

LAST TIME ?

NO

YES

of the lowest memory location that contained the data, and incremented by one until the last memory location containing data had been processed.

Multiplication

Although some of the more powerful microcomputers have a "built-in" hardware multiplication circuit in their ALU, most multiplication is still performed by software. The program is actually a sequence of steps designed to perform the multiplication according to a binary algorithm. (The term *algorithm* is really synonymous with "procedure" and implies that the desired operation must be done in small steps leading toward the end product.)

The first step is to choose a multiplication algorithm that can be suitably programmed to provide all the requirements of the application. One most important consideration is that the "product" of the two numbers multiplied together will have as many digits as the sum of the digits of the two numbers. (Zeros may occur on the left-hand side.) Also, the magnitude of the product of the two numbers may easily exceed the range of an 8-bit data word, and it may be necessary to write a more complex program, using two words to store each of the numbers. Furthermore, we must consider the requirements that are necessary for keeping track of the sign (+ or −) of the product.

Clearly, we can see that this "simple" task of multiplying two numbers, using software, can get quite complex. We will therefore discuss the concept within a limited set of rules.

1. The multiplicand and the multiplier will always be positive numbers.
2. The numeric value of the multiplicand and the multiplier shall not exceed 15_{DEC} (1111_{BIN}), and therefore may be stored in only 4 bits.

Now, the multiplication algorithm that we will use is stated below.

(1) Test the least significant bit (LSB) of the multiplier for 1 or 0.
    (a) If it is 1, add the multiplicand to the result (initialized to zero). Then go to (2).
    (b) If it is 0, go to (2).
(2) Shift the multiplicand to the left, one bit.
(3) Shift the multiplier to the right, one bit, and go back to (1).

A simplified flowchart of this procedure is shown in Fig. 4-15.

Let's go through an example of the use of the algorithm, using the problem $9 \times 11 = 99$.

R   = 00000000   First we must initialize the result to zero.
MC = 00001011   The multiplicand, 11_{DEC}.

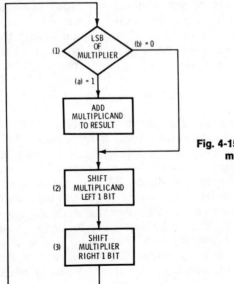

Fig. 4-15. Simple flowchart of binary multiplication algorithm.

MP = 00001001	The multiplier, 9_{DEC}.	
R = 00001011	LSB = 1; add multiplicand to result, 11_{DEC}.	
MC = 00010110	Shift multiplicand left one bit, 22_{DEC}.	
MP = 00000100	Shift multiplier right one bit, 4_{DEC}.	
	LSB = 0.	
MC = 00101100	Shift multiplicand left one bit, 44_{DEC}.	
MP = 00000010	Shift multiplier right one bit, 2_{DEC}.	
	LSB = 0.	
MC = 01011000	Shift multiplicand left one bit, 88_{DEC}.	
MP = 00000001	Shift multiplier right one bit, 1_{DEC}.	
R = 01100011	LSB = 1; add multiplicand to result, 99_{DEC}.	

There are a few more steps that must be added to the algorithm if it is to be programmed for execution by a computer. First of all, the multiplicand and the multiplier must be located at some specific address in memory. There must also be a designated memory location in which the result (product of the multiplication) is to be stored. The reader may also have observed that the very first thing that has to be done is to initialize the result to zero. Then, each time that the LSB of the multiplier is 1, the multiplicand is added to the result, until the last bit of the multiplier has been tested. This introduces an interesting question: How will the computer know when the last multiplier bit has been tested? The program must supply this information by keeping track of which bit of the multiplier is currently being examined. To accomplish this, we may use a word in memory to store the number of the bit (NB) being examined. This must be initialized to one, and then be incremented by one, after each bit is tested, until it is equal to four, which will signal the program that the multiplication is completed. Fig. 4-16 shows an expanded flowchart of the program.

Table Search Routines

Rather than involving a lot of data, some computer applications may involve a complex process that uses only a few elements of data during execution. Others, especially those relating to some sort of data processing operation, will most likely involve many elements of data. One thing we must remember at this point is that the computer, though having memory, does not have a mind. It doesn't know how to spell nor does it even know the letters of the English alphabet. It can be told to add 2 + 2, but must also be told what "2" is. This almost constant need for a catalog of information is filled by a programming

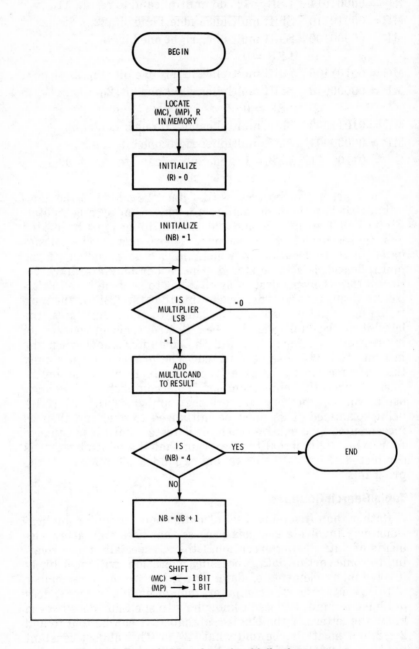

Fig. 4-16. Expanded flowchart of multiplication program.

technique known as *data tables* and the related *table search routines*.

As an example, a data table may be used in a computer system employing an ASCII keyboard as an input device. As a key is depressed, the keyboard interface encodes it into binary code. Once transferred into the memory of the computer, the binary code must be analyzed by some program to determine which character it represents. In doing so, the program may scan a table of all the possible characters, comparing each one to the character that was input, until a match occurs.

To carry the example one step further, consider the following. Suppose that part of the processing required that the input character be converted from the ASCII code to some other form of character encoding, such as Baudot (the old-style five-level Teletype code). For this, we could set up a second data table that would contain all of the Baudot character codes in the same sequence as the ASCII table. Then, when the input character was matched with an entry in the ASCII table, the corresponding entry in the Baudot table would provide the converted code.

These tables are usually in the form of areas of the memory that incorporate any number of sequential memory locations. Then, accessing of these memory locations can be controlled by a register in the CPU which "points" to the particular entry in the table. This register can then be incremented, or decremented, as it is used with instructions in the pointer register relative addressing mode. Of course, if there are going to be several tables used in conjunction with one another, there will have to be several registers to manage them.

Tables of this type are known as *sequential access* tables because they are usable only by starting at the beginning (or low-order end of the table) and proceeding through the entries in an ascending sequence to the high-order end of the table. This technique is quite adequate as long as the size of the table is kept fairly small. The computing time required to fully scan a large table would soon become a detriment to the operation of the overall program. In this regard, there are "faster" table search routines that don't have to start at the beginning of the table but can start at some likely point in the middle of the table. This likely point must be determined by the program based on some predefined rules regarding the information that is to be stored in the table. The details of these routines exceed the scope of this book, and the reader should, at this point, be aware of their existence and their usefulness. At this time, we shall remain with the sequential search technique as used for the ASCII to Baudot conversion.

As shown in Fig. 4-17, there are two tables in memory. One contains the characters of the alphabet in ASCII code, while the other contains the same alphabet in Baudot code. Once the input character has been read and is ready to be converted, the routine begins with the initializing of address pointers A and B. Pointer A is set to the memory address that contains the first entry of the ASCII table. According to the memory map shown in the illustration, this would be a hexadecimal value of 0120. Also, the B pointer is set equal to the memory address that contains the first entry of the Baudot table. This would be the hexadecimal value of 0190. The next step, then, is to compare the input character with the first entry in the ASCII table, to determine if they do match. If the two characters do not match, then the program must determine if the end of the table has been reached. This can be accomplished by comparing the A pointer register value to the address that represents the last entry in the table. This, according to the memory map, is

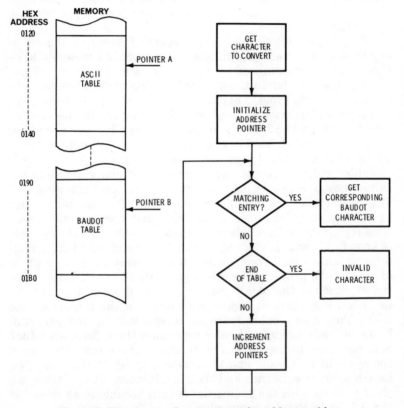

Fig. 4-17. Flowchart and memory map for table searching.

the hexadecimal value 0140. If the A pointer register does not contain this value, then the end of the table has not yet been reached, and both the A and B pointer registers are incremented by one. This will make them "point" at the next entry in the tables. The program then goes back to compare the input character with the next table entry, and so on, until either a match is found or the end of the table is reached. If the end of the table is reached and no match has been found, then the input character must then be an invalid ASCII character and some provision must be made for the program to handle this situation.

Notice that here we have not only an example of table searching, but also another example of the iteration process.

WRITING A PROGRAM

Regardless of the particular computer being used, or the programming language, there are some general ideas that are common to most programming tasks. In some cases, the programming task may become noticeably difficult, especially when the upper limit of the computer's features is approached. For example, some of the lower-power microprocessors will only allow addressing of memory locations that are within a rather small range of the location of the instruction that is doing the addressing. This means that if the program itself is to be large, any memory locations that contain data for the program will most likely have to be addressed through the use of a hardware pointer register (a premium commodity to the programmer). This same program task, when programmed on a higher-power microprocessor, can be done with ease. These higher-power microprocessors allow direct addressing of any word in a memory up to 64K.

So, there are many differences between the approaches that a programmer might use when dealing with a high-, or low-power processor. However, if we were to observe a programmer working at a programming job, we would not always be able to tell whether the job was for a high-power, or a low-power machine. There are certain things that need to be done, and in a definite sequence, no matter what the machine. These are what we will explore in this section as we program a Motorola MC6800 microprocessor to do a very simple task.

Sequential Description

The very first thing that the programmer must do is to define exactly what the computer's task is. This should begin as a simple statement, and then be expanded as the programmer develops the approach. For our example program, we will define its purpose:

To MOVE the contents of one area of memory into another area of memory.

Of course, these areas of memory have been designated for the storage of some sort of data. The object of our program is to create an exact duplicate of the first area and place it in the other area of memory. At this point we should recall the discussion regarding the memory map. Fig. 4-18 is a duplicate of the memory map that pertains to this programming job.

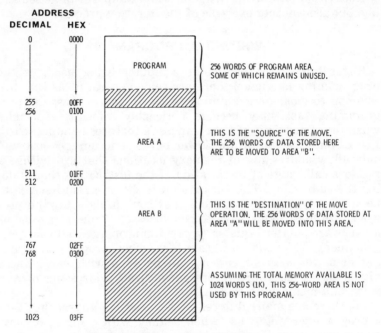

Fig. 4-18. Memory map for MOVE program.

Recall that this MOVE program is going to be written for execution on a Motorola MC6800 microprocessor equipped with 1K of read/write memory. As we see in the memory map, the first 256 words of the 1K memory are reserved for the program itself. The second 256 words of the memory are allocated for the A area. This is the "origin" of the MOVE operation. It consists of the data that are to be moved into the B area, or "destination." The B area is located in the third block of 256 words in the 1K memory. The fourth block of 256 words is not used by this program.

Now we know where everything is located in the memory, and we have a general idea of what the program is to do. At this point, we can become more specific. We begin with a list of the basic operations that must occur in order to realize the defined purpose of the program. This list would start as follows:

1. LOAD a word from area A into the accumulator.
2. STORE the word in area B.
3. END after doing these steps 256 times.

Here we have the three most basic elements of this program. We can see from this list that we are going to be using "memory access" instructions to LOAD and STORE these words. These instructions require that the operand (the object of the action of the instruction) be defined as a memory address at the time the instruction is to be executed. Therefore, we will need to keep track of memory addresses for both the A and B areas.

The easiest way to fulfill this requirement is to make use of the MC6800's extended addressing mode. In this mode, the operand address is specified in the two words immediately following the word in the program that contains the instruction. So, the two words directly following the LOAD instruction will specify the address of the A area word to be loaded into the accumulator. Likewise, the two words directly following the STORE instruction will specify the address of the word in area B that is to receive the contents of the accumulator. Since these words following the instructions can be treated as just another memory location, they too can be modified during the execution of the program, so that the address that they specify can be changed. Each time that a word is transferred from area A into area B, the program must also modify these addresses by adding one, thereby "pointing" them to the next word in both areas.

Another consideration at this time is how to determine when the full 256 words have been moved and when it is time for the program to end. This brings back our old friend, "iteration." We will need to initialize a counter of some sort, increment it each time a word is moved, and test it to see if the total 256 words have been moved. For this, we can also use just another word of memory. It will be initialized to zero before the program begins and then incremented by one each time that a word of data is moved from area A into area B. Since the MC6800 is an 8-bit device, the largest unsigned binary number that can be stored in one word is 255. If this value is incremented, as it will be after the last data word has been moved, all the bits of the word will be cleared to zero, and the zero condition bit in the status register will be set to one. So, to test the counter to determine when the last data word has been moved, we need only test for all zeros, which will indicate that the counter has just been incremented from 255 to 256. When this occurs, the move operation will be complete, and the program can be ended with a HALT instruction.

Now, we can expand the sequential description further as in the following:

1. CLEAR the counter to zero.
2. LOAD (extended) a word from area A into the accumulator.
3. STORE (extended) the word in area B.
4. INCREMENT the counter by one.
5. TEST the counter. If zero, GO TO (8).
6. INCREMENT area A address and area B address.
7. GO TO (2).
8. HALT.

There is one last thing to consider. The extended-mode LOAD and STORE instructions that transfer the data from the A area to the B area find the operand memory address contained in the two words immediately following the instruction in the program. The first of these words contains the most significant bits (MSBs) of the memory address, and the second word contains the least significant bits (LSBs) of the address. The two words, linked together, form a 16-bit unsigned binary number, which is the absolute address of the operand. In order to increment these addresses, a one is added to the second word of the pair (LSB). Now, at some point, this second word may possibly contain all 1 bits (255_{DEC}). If we add a one to this word, it will result in an arithmetic carry, clearing all the bits in the word to zero and setting the zero condition bit in the status register. At this point, we must now increment the first word of the address pair that contains the most significant bits (MSBs). It is obvious that incrementing the addresses will require several instructions. At this time the sequential description appears as follows:

1. CLEAR the counter to zero.
2. LOAD (extended) a word from area A into the accumulator.
3. STORE (extended) the word in area B.
4. INCREMENT the counter by one.
5. TEST the counter. If zero, GO TO (13).
6. INCREMENT the LSB of the area A address.

7. TEST the LSB portion. If not zero, GO TO (9).
8. INCREMENT the MSB portion of the area A address.
9. INCREMENT the LSB of the area B address.
10. TEST the LSB portion. If not zero, GO TO (2).
11. INCREMENT the MSB portion of the area B address.
12. GO TO (2).
13. HALT.

Note here that this program has been designed for the sake of illustration of the programming steps. The beginning A and B area addresses will be "built into" the LOAD and STORE instructions as we hand-assemble the program later in this section. After the program has finished execution, the processor will simply stop. This is not the usual method of programming a computer, since most computers are not dedicated solely to such simple tasks as moving data from one place in the memory to another.

Flowcharting

Flowcharting is the most often neglected element of the programming task. By the time the programmer has come this far in the development of the program, he does not really need a flowchart to know what his program is doing. The designer of a program is so intimately involved with the program that he knows all the "ins and outs" and the "whys and wherefores" of every instruction. What most programmers fail to think about is that perhaps someday in the future, some other programmer will have to sit down and try to figure out how the program works.

This, then, is the primary reason for flowcharting: to document the logical operation of the program in a way that can be understood by any programmer. This can save great amounts of time and trouble if for some reason the program is inherited by a programmer unfamiliar with it.

Some would argue that this is not the time to draw a flowchart of the program, since subsequent testing of the program might reveal a logic error which would necessitate the modification of the program. They might say that it would be better to wait until the program had been thoroughly checked out and tested before the flowchart was drawn. This sounds great, except for the inevitable situation in which the programmer is halfway finished with a program, and suddenly disappears in search of more money, a bigger computer, more important assignments, and so on.

So, at least a rough flowchart should be drawn at this time. It doesn't have to be a work of art, but it should be neat and readable and of course disclose any parts of the program that may not be readily noticed. Later, after the final program has been accepted, a final flowchart can be drawn to replace this working drawing.

There are really only two shapes that are predominant in flowchart drawings. The rectangle represents some process to be done by the CPU. The diamond represents a decision to be made, usually based on the result of some process. The outcome of the decision may result in the rerouting of the program, indicated by the arrows connecting the rectangles and diamonds. Some sort of description should be written inside (or alongside) the flowchart elements to indicate the operation they represent. Also, since the sequential description of the program will already have numbered steps, these same numbers can be transcribed onto the flowchart in the appropriate positions. Fig. 4-19 is a flowchart of the program which is described in this section.

Instruction Sequence

By using the sequential description of the program and the flowchart drawing to help visualize the overall nature of the program, we can determine the actual CPU instructions. Of course, we have had these instructions in mind ever since we first started to design the program. The fact that the MC6800 CPU accommodates an extended addressing mode means that the two data areas can be addressed through the use of a two-word operand that follows the instructions. The MC6800 instruction set also offers increment and decrement instructions (INC and DEC), making the task of maintaining a counter a simple one. Finally, the basic arithmetic logic of the MC6800 led to the "testing for zero" concept used in incrementing the area addresses, as well as in determining when 256 words had been moved.

Next we will use the information provided by the manufacturer. This information describes each of the instructions from a hardware standpoint. Fig. 4-20 is a reproduction of the Instruction Set Summary card provided by Motorola Corp. for the MC6800 chip. Using this, we will construct the basic framework of the program. We will begin by writing down the mnemonics (abbreviations) for each of the instructions, in the order that they are to executed. Realizing that each instruction must have some sort of operand, we will also write in a name designating the object of the operation. Also, for each instruction, we will write a short description (similar to the sequential description) of the operation which is performed in the computer.

As an example, we will now work through Table 4-1, one step at a time, while using the sequential description as a guide and the Instruction Set Summary card. Observe the following:

First, at Step (1) we must clear the counter to zero. This counter is to be a word in memory, located near the program. Its actual address can be determined later, so for now we will use the CLR instruction with a symbolic operand called COUNTER. This instruction will set all the bits in the operand to 0.

In Step (2), we must load a word from the A area into the accumulator. We decided to use the extended addressing mode, which will specify the address of the operand in the two words

Table 4-1. Instruction Sequence for the MOVE Program

Step	Label	Mnemonic	Operand	Description
1		CLR	COUNTER	Clear the counter to zero
2	MOVE	LDAA	AREAA	Load accumulator A with a word from data area A
3		STAA	AREAB	Store accumulator A in a word in data area B
4		INC	COUNTER	Increment the counter by one
5		BEQ	HALT	Branch to HALT if counter became zero
6		INC	LSBA	Increment the LSB of the address for data area A by one
7		BNE	INCB	Branch if not equal to zero to increment area B address
8		INC	MSBA	Increment the MSB of the A area address
9	INCB	INC	LSBB	Increment the LSB of the address for data area B by one
10		BNE	MOVE	Branch if not equal to zero to MOVE another word
11		INC	MSBB	Otherwise, increment MSB of B area address
12		BRA	MOVE	Then branch always to MOVE another word
13	HALT	WAI		This is the HALT for the program

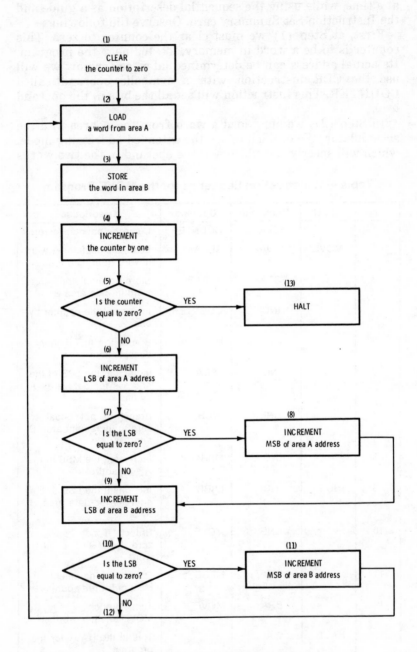

Fig. 4-19. Flowchart of the MOVE program.

(1) CLEAR the counter to zero

(2) LOAD a word from area A

(3) STORE the word in area B

(4) INCREMENT the counter by one

(5) Is the counter equal to zero?

(13) HALT

(6) INCREMENT LSB of area A address

(7) Is the LSB equal to zero?

(8) INCREMENT MSB of area A address

(9) INCREMENT LSB of area B address

(10) Is the LSB equal to zero?

(11) INCREMENT MSB of area B address

(12)

immediately following the instruction word. Again, the actual address will be worked out later. Since the MC6800 has two accumulators, we will elect to use the A accumulator only. Looking at the Instruction Set Summary card, we find that the instruction we wish to use is called LDAA. For now, we will simply refer to the operand symbolically as AREAA, the A area. Notice here the "label" that has been attached in Table 4-1 to this instruction: MOVE. This point in the program is where the MOVE operation begins. It is "branched" to, as we see on the flowchart, for each word to be moved, until all 256 have been moved. Therefore, we must have some way of referencing this particular instruction. Hence, the symbolic label, MOVE.

In Step (3), once the word from area A has been loaded into the accumulator, it must be stored in the B area. To do this, we will use another extended addressing mode instruction, STAA. Also, the symbolic operand AREAB is assigned at this time. The actual memory location address will be figured later.

Now that the program has just moved one word from area A into area B, Step (4) says we must increment the counter by one. The MC6800 instruction set conveniently includes an instruction just for this purpose. It is called INC, and it will add one to the specified operand. The operand in this case of course is COUNTER, which was set to zero at Step (1). Now, if the 256th word has just been moved, the COUNTER prior to being incremented will equal 11111111 (255 in unsigned binary). Adding one to this binary number will cause all the bits to be set to zero, and the zero condition bit in the status register will also be set. This offers a simple way of testing to see if all 256 words have been moved. If the COUNTER value is ever equal to zero after it is incremented, we know that it has been incremented for the 256th time, and the job is finished. We will use a *conditional branch* instruction called BEQ (branch if equal to zero) to cause the program to branch to the address specified in the operand. In this case, we will assign the symbolic operand HALT. This will be an instruction, somewhere in the program, that will cause the CPU to stop.

If the COUNTER is not equal to zero, then there are more words to be moved, and at Step (6) we begin to increment the data area addresses. This operation can also make use of the INC instruction, except that in this case the operand will be the LSB of the A area address. Since this is actually the second word following the LDAA instruction at Step (2), we will assign the symbolic name LSBA to the operand at this time. Here again, we will make use of the same fact that if arithmetic overflow has occurred, the contents of the LSB of the A area address will be equal to zero after it is incremented. If this is true, then we will also have to increment the MSB of the area A address.

In Step (7), we will use another conditional branch instruction to cause the program to ignore the MSB incrementing op-

ACCUMULATOR AND MEMORY OPERATIONS	MNEMONIC	IMMED OP	~	#	DIRECT OP	~	#	INDEX OP	~	#	EXTND OP	~	#	INHER OP	~	#	BOOLEAN/ARITHMETIC OPERATION (All register labels refer to contents)	H (5)	I (4)	N (3)	Z (2)	V (1)	C (0)
Add	ADDA	8B	2	2	9B	3	2	AB	5	2	BB	4	3					A+M→A	↕	•	↕	↕	↕	↕
	ADDB	CB	2	2	DB	3	2	EB	5	2	FB	4	3					B+M→B	↕	•	↕	↕	↕	↕
Add Acmltrs	ABA													1B	2	1	A+B→A	↕	•	↕	↕	↕	↕
Add with Carry	ADCA	89	2	2	99	3	2	A9	5	2	B9	4	3				A+M+C→A	↕	•	↕	↕	↕	↕
	ADCB	C9	2	2	D9	3	2	E9	5	2	F9	4	3				B+M+C→B	↕	•	↕	↕	↕	↕
And	ANDA	84	2	2	94	3	2	A4	5	2	B4	4	3				A•M→A	•	•	↕	↕	R	•
	ANDB	C4	2	2	D4	3	2	E4	5	2	F4	4	3				B•M→B	•	•	↕	↕	R	•
Bit Test	BITA	85	2	2	95	3	2	A5	5	2	B5	4	3				A•M	•	•	↕	↕	R	•
	BITB	C5	2	2	D5	3	2	E5	5	2	F5	4	3				B•M	•	•	↕	↕	R	•
Clear	CLR							6F	7	2	7F	6	3				00→M	•	•	R	S	R	R
	CLRA													4F	2	1	00→A	•	•	R	S	R	R
	CLRB													5F	2	1	00→B	•	•	R	S	R	R
Compare	CMPA	81	2	2	91	3	2	A1	5	2	B1	4	3				A-M	•	•	↕	↕	↕	↕
	CMPB	C1	2	2	D1	3	2	E1	5	2	F1	4	3				B-M	•	•	↕	↕	↕	↕
Compare Acmltrs	CBA													11	2	1	A-B	•	•	↕	↕	↕	↕
Complement, 1's	COM							63	7	2	73	6	3				M̄→M	•	•	↕	↕	R	S
	COMA													43	2	1	Ā→A	•	•	↕	↕	R	S
	COMB													53	2	1	B̄→B	•	•	↕	↕	R	S
Complement, 2's (Negate)	NEG							60	7	2	70	6	3				00-M→M	•	•	↕	↕	①	②
	NEGA													40	2	1	00-A→A	•	•	↕	↕	①	②
	NEGB													50	2	1	00-B→B	•	•	↕	↕	①	②
Decimal Adjust, A	DAA													19	2	1	Converts Binary Add. of BCD Characters into BCD Format	•	•	↕	↕	↕	③
Decrement	DEC							6A	7	2	7A	6	3				M-1→M	•	•	↕	↕	④	•
	DECA													4A	2	1	A-1→A	•	•	↕	↕	④	•
	DECB													5A	2	1	B-1→B	•	•	↕	↕	④	•
Exclusive OR	EORA	88	2	2	98	3	2	A8	5	2	B8	4	3				A⊕M→A	•	•	↕	↕	R	•
	EORB	C8	2	2	D8	3	2	E8	5	2	F8	4	3				B⊕M→B	•	•	↕	↕	R	•
Increment	INC							6C	7	2	7C	6	3				M+1→M	•	•	↕	↕	⑤	•
	INCA													4C	2	1	A+1→A	•	•	↕	↕	⑤	•
	INCB													5C	2	1	B+1→B	•	•	↕	↕	⑤	•
Load Acmltr	LDAA	86	2	2	96	3	2	A6	5	2	B6	4	3				M→A	•	•	↕	↕	R	•
	LDAB	C6	2	2	D6	3	2	E6	5	2	F6	4	3				M→B	•	•	↕	↕	R	•
Or, Inclusive	ORAA	8A	2	2	9A	3	2	AA	5	2	BA	4	3				A+M→A	•	•	↕	↕	R	•
	ORAB	CA	2	2	DA	3	2	EA	5	2	FA	4	3				B+M→B	•	•	↕	↕	R	•
Push Data	PSHA													36	4	1	A→Msp, SP-1→SP	•	•	•	•	•	•
	PSHB													37	4	1	B→Msp, SP-1→SP	•	•	•	•	•	•
Pull Data	PULA													32	4	1	SP+1→SP, Msp→A	•	•	•	•	•	•
	PULB													33	4	1	SP+1→SP, Msp→B	•	•	•	•	•	•
Rotate Left	ROL							69	7	2	79	6	3				M	•	•	↕	↕	⑥	↕
	ROLA													49	2	1	A 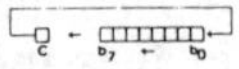	•	•	↕	↕	⑥	↕
	ROLB													59	2	1	B	•	•	↕	↕	⑥	↕
Rotate Right	ROR							66	7	2	76	6	3				M	•	•	↕	↕	⑥	↕
	RORA													46	2	1	A 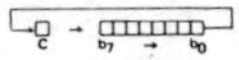	•	•	↕	↕	⑥	↕
	RORB													56	2	1	B	•	•	↕	↕	⑥	↕
Shift Left, Arithmetic	ASL							68	7	2	78	6	3				M	•	•	↕	↕	⑥	↕
	ASLA													48	2	1	A 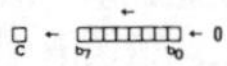	•	•	↕	↕	⑥	↕
	ASLB													58	2	1	B	•	•	↕	↕	⑥	↕
Shift Right, Arithmetic	ASR							67	7	2	77	6	3				M	•	•	↕	↕	⑥	↕
	ASRA													47	2	1	A 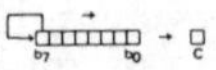	•	•	↕	↕	⑥	↕
	ASRB													57	2	1	B	•	•	↕	↕	⑥	↕
Shift Right, Logic	LSR							64	7	2	74	6	3				M	•	•	R	↕	⑥	↕
	LSRA													44	2	1	A 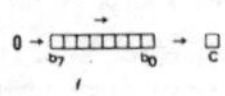	•	•	R	↕	⑥	↕
	LSRB													54	2	1	B	•	•	R	↕	⑥	↕
Store Acmltr	STAA				97	4	2	A7	6	2	B7	5	3				A→M	•	•	↕	↕	R	•
	STAB				D7	4	2	E7	6	2	F7	5	3				B→M	•	•	↕	↕	R	•
Subtract	SUBA	80	2	2	90	3	2	A0	5	2	B0	4	3				A-M→A	•	•	↕	↕	↕	↕
	SUBB	C0	2	2	D0	3	2	E0	5	2	F0	4	3				B-M→B	•	•	↕	↕	↕	↕
Subract Acmltrs	SBA													10	2	1	A-B→A	•	•	↕	↕	↕	↕
Subtr. with Carry	SBCA	82	2	2	92	3	2	A2	5	2	B2	4	3				A-M-C→A	•	•	↕	↕	↕	↕
	SBCB	C2	2	2	D2	3	2	E2	5	2	F2	4	3				B-M-C→B	•	•	↕	↕	↕	↕
Transfer Acmltrs	TAB													16	2	1	A→B	•	•	↕	↕	R	•
	TBA													17	2	1	B→A	•	•	↕	↕	R	•
Test, Zero or Minus	TST							6D	7	2	7D	6	3				M-00	•	•	↕	↕	R	R
	TSTA													4D	2	1	A-00	•	•	↕	↕	R	R
	TSTB													5D	2	1	B-00	•	•	↕	↕	R	R

Fig. 4-20. MC6800 Instruction

eration if the LSB is not equal to zero. The instruction is called BNE (branch if not equal to zero). So, if the LSB of the A area address is not zero after it is incremented, the program will branch to the address specified by the operand of the BNE instruction. Since this will be some other part of the program,

INDEX REGISTER AND STACK POINTER OPERATIONS	MNEMONIC	IMMED OP	~	#	DIRECT OP	~	#	INDEX OP	~	#	EXTND OP	~	#	INHER OP	~	#	BOOLEAN/ARITHMETIC OPERATION	5 H	4 I	3 N	2 Z	1 V	0 C
Compare Index Reg	CPX	8C	3	3	9C	4	2	AC	6	2	BC	5	3				$(X_H/X_L) - (M/M+1)$	•	•	⑦	↕	⑧	•
Decrement Index Reg	DEX													09	4	1	$X - 1 \rightarrow X$	•	•	•	↕	•	•
Decrement Stack Pntr	DES													34	4	1	$SP - 1 \rightarrow SP$	•	•	•	•	•	•
Increment Index Reg	INX													08	4	1	$X + 1 \rightarrow X$	•	•	•	↕	•	•
Increment Stack Pntr	INS													31	4	1	$SP + 1 \rightarrow SP$	•	•	•	•	•	•
Load Index Reg	LDX	CE	3	3	DE	4	2	EE	6	2	FE	5	3				$M \rightarrow X_H, (M+1) \rightarrow X_L$	•	•	⑨	↕	R	•
Load Stack Pntr	LDS	8E	3	3	9E	4	2	AE	6	2	BE	5	3				$M \rightarrow SP_H, (M+1) \rightarrow SP_L$	•	•	⑨	↕	R	•
Store Index Reg	STX				DF	5	2	EF	7	2	FF	6	3				$X_H \rightarrow M, X_L \rightarrow (M+1)$	•	•	⑨	↕	R	•
Store Stack Pntr	STS				9F	5	2	AF	7	2	BF	6	3				$SP_H \rightarrow M, SP_L \rightarrow (M+1)$	•	•	⑨	↕	R	•
Indx Reg → Stack Pntr	TXS													35	4	1	$X - 1 \rightarrow SP$	•	•	•	•	•	•
Stack Pntr → Indx Reg	TSX													30	4	1	$SP + 1 \rightarrow X$	•	•	•	•	•	•

JUMP AND BRANCH OPERATIONS	MNEMONIC	RELATIVE OP	~	#	INDEX OP	~	#	EXTND OP	~	#	INHER OP	~	#	BRANCH TEST	5 H	4 I	3 N	2 Z	1 V	0 C
Branch Always	BRA	20	4	2										None	•	•	•	•	•	•
Branch If Carry Clear	BCC	24	4	2										$C = 0$	•	•	•	•	•	•
Branch If Carry Set	BCS	25	4	2										$C = 1$	•	•	•	•	•	•
Branch If = Zero	BEQ	27	4	2										$Z = 1$	•	•	•	•	•	•
Branch If ≥ Zero	BGE	2C	4	2										$N \oplus V = 0$	•	•	•	•	•	•
Branch If > Zero	BGT	2E	4	2										$Z + (N \oplus V) = 0$	•	•	•	•	•	•
Branch If Higher	BHI	22	4	2										$C + Z = 0$	•	•	•	•	•	•
Branch If ≤ Zero	BLE	2F	4	2										$Z + (N \oplus V) = 1$	•	•	•	•	•	•
Branch If Lower Or Same	BLS	23	4	2										$C + Z = 1$	•	•	•	•	•	•
Branch If < Zero	BLT	2D	4	2										$N \oplus V = 1$	•	•	•	•	•	•
Branch If Minus	BMI	2B	4	2										$N = 1$	•	•	•	•	•	•
Branch If Not Equal Zero	BNE	26	4	2										$Z = 0$	•	•	•	•	•	•
Branch If Overflow Clear	BVC	28	4	2										$V = 0$	•	•	•	•	•	•
Branch If Overflow Set	BVS	29	4	2										$V = 1$	•	•	•	•	•	•
Branch If Plus	BPL	2A	4	2										$N = 0$	•	•	•	•	•	•
Branch To Subroutine	BSR	8D	8	2											•	•	•	•	•	•
Jump	JMP				6E	4	2	7E	3	3				See Special Operations	•	•	•	•	•	•
Jump To Subroutine	JSR				AD	8	2	BD	9	3					•	•	•	•	•	•
No Operation	NOP										01	2	1	Advances Prog. Cntr. Only	•	•	•	•	•	•
Return From Interrupt	RTI										3B	10	1		— ⑩ —
Return From Subroutine	RTS										39	5	1	See special Operations	•	•	•	•	•	•
Software Interrupt	SWI										3F	12	1		•	S	•	•	•	•
Wait for Interrupt	WAI										3E	9	1		•	⑬	•	•	•	•

CONDITIONS CODE REGISTER OPERATIONS	MNEMONIC	INHER OP	~	=	BOOLEAN OPERATION	5 H	4 I	3 N	2 Z	1 V	0 C
Clear Carry	CLC	0C	2	1	$0 \rightarrow C$	•	•	•	•	•	R
Clear Interrupt Mask	CLI	0E	2	1	$0 \rightarrow I$	•	R	•	•	•	•
Clear Overflow	CLV	0A	2	1	$0 \rightarrow V$	•	•	•	•	R	•
Set Carry	SEC	0D	2	1	$1 \rightarrow C$	•	•	•	•	•	S
Set Interrupt Mask	SEI	0F	2	1	$1 \rightarrow I$	•	S	•	•	•	•
Set Overflow	SEV	0B	2	1	$1 \rightarrow V$	•	•	•	•	S	•
Acmltr A → CCR	TAP	06	2	1	$A \rightarrow CCR$	— ⑫ —
CCR → Acmltr A	TPA	07	2	1	$CCR \rightarrow A$	•	•	•	•	•	•

CONDITION CODE REGISTER NOTES:

(Bit set if test is true and cleared otherwise)

① (Bit V) Test: Result = 10000000?
② (Bit C) Test: Result = 00000000?
③ (Bit C) Test: Decimal value of most significant BCD Character greater than nine? (Not cleared if previously set.)
④ (Bit V) Test: Operand = 10000000 prior to execution?
⑤ (Bit V) Test: Operand = 01111111 prior to execution?
⑥ (Bit V) Test: Set equal to result of N ⊕ C after shift has occurred.
⑦ (Bit N) Test: Sign bit of most significant (MS) byte of result = 1?
⑧ (Bit V) Test: 2's complement overflow from subtraction of LS bytes?
⑨ (Bit N) Test: Result less than zero? (Bit 15 = 1)
⑩ (All) Load Condition Code Register from Stack. (See Special Operations)
⑬ (Bit I) Set when interrupt occurs. If previously set, a Non-Maskable Interrupt is required to exit the wait state.
⑬ (ALL) Set according to the contents of Accumulator A.

LEGEND:

OP	Operation Code (Hexadecimal);		00	Byte = Zero;
~	Number of MPU Cycles;		H	Half-carry from bit 3;
=	Number of Program Bytes;		I	Interrupt mask
+	Arithmetic Plus;		N	Negative (sign bit)
–	Arithmetic Minus;		Z	Zero (byte)
•	Boolean AND;		V	Overflow, 2's complement
M_{SP}	Contents of memory location pointed to be Stack Pointer;		C	Carry from bit 7
			R	Reset Always
+	Boolean Inclusive OR;		S	Set Always
⊕	Boolean Exclusive OR;		↕	Test and set if true, cleared otherwise
$\overline{M}$	Complement of M;		•	Not Affected
→	Transfer Into;		CCR	Condition Code Register
0	Bit = Zero;		LS	Least Significant
			MS	Most Significant

Set Summary card.

Table 4-2. Hand-Assembled Instruction Sequence for MOVE

Step	Address	Word	Label	Mnemonic	Operand	Description
1	0000	7F	COUNTER	CLR	COUNTER	This word is used for COUNTER (The remaining descriptions are the same as in Table 4-1)
	0001	00				
	0002	00				
	0003	00				
2	0004	B6	MOVE	LDAA	AREAA	
	0005	01				
	0006	00				
3	0007	B7		STAA	AREAB	
	0008	02				
	0009	00				
4	000A	7C		INC	COUNTER	
	000B	00				
	000C	00				
5	000D	27		BEQ	HALT	
	000E	12				
6	000F	7C		INC	LSBA	
	0010	00				
	0011	06				

7	0012	26		BNE	INCB
	0013	03			
8	0014	7C		INC	MSBA
	0015	00			
	0016	05			
9	0017	7C	INCB	INC	LSBB
	0018	00			
	0019	09			
10	001A	26		BNE	MOVE
	001B	E8			
11	001C	7C		INC	MSBB
	001D	00			
	001E	08			
12	001F	20		BRA	MOVE
	0020	E3			
13	0021	3E	HALT	WAI	

we will assign the symbolic name INCB as the operand for now and work out the exact memory address later.

However, if the result of incrementing the LSB of the A area address yields a value of zero, the program will not branch at Step (7) but will proceed to execute the instruction at Step (8). This instruction is the INC operation to be performed on the MSB of the A area address. Again, since we are still dealing in symbolic terms, we will assign the operand called MSBA.

Step (9) is the first part of the incrementing of the B area address. Here again, we begin by first using the INC instruction to increment the LSB of the B area address. The symbolic operand LSBB is assigned to this instruction. The same principle applies here: if arithmetic carry occurs as a result of incrementing the LSB of the B area address, a value of zero will be contained in the address word; otherwise, the result will be nonzero.

In Step (10), we observe the same type of testing of the LSB of the B area address. The BNE instruction (branch if not equal to zero) causes the program to branch back to the MOVE label if no arithmetic carry has occurred.

If the contents of the LSB of the B area address are zero after it is incremented, then the program will proceed to execute the instruction at Step (11). The MSB of the B area address is incremented by using the same INC instruction. Again, we have assigned the symbolic name MSBB as the operand.

In Step (12), we must branch back to the beginning of the MOVE operation. The addresses have been incremented, and it is now time to move another word. Since this is a branch that must always be made, we will use the instruction called BRA (branch always) to cause the program to go back to the address specified in the operand. This, of course, is the symbolic label MOVE.

Step (13) is the instruction that is to be executed when the entire 256 words have been moved from area A into area B. Here we have used the instruction called WAI (wait), which will cause the CPU to stop executing instructions. This marks the end of the program and bears the symbolic label HALT.

Hand Assembly

Now that the instruction sequence has been established, we may proceed to determine the actual memory addresses of the instructions, as well as the binary bit patterns that represent the instructions themselves. Rather than use binary notation, however, we will use the hexadecimal abbreviation of binary. Referring to the manufacturer's Instruction Set Summary card once again, we see that here, too, the hexadecimal notation is used to designate the equivalent binary bit pattern for the instruction. There are several approaches to the hand-assembly task, any one of which is probably just as valid as the next. The object, of course, is to produce a functional program in the least amount of time, with the least amount of frustration for the programmer.

For the purpose of this illustration, we will add two more columns to the instruction sequence shown in Table 4-1. These two columns will be added between the Step and Label columns, and will be called "Address" and "Word," respectively. The Address column will contain the memory addresses, in sequential order, beginning with the first word of the program. The word column will contain the hexadecimal representation of the contents of the memory locations. In reality, these two columns should be planned for when the instruction sequence is determined. However, for simplicity's sake, they were not introduced into our illustration until now.

Remembering that a word of memory is to be used for the COUNTER, and also that the first instruction to be executed is the one that is contained in memory location 0001, we will assign the counter to be contained in memory the location 0000. The actual contents of the COUNTER are of no consequence, since it is cleared to zero as the program begins.

Memory location 0001 contains the first instruction of the program. This is the CLR instruction that is to clear the COUNTER to zero. From the Instruction Set Summary card, we see that this instruction may be used in either the indexed or the extended addressing modes. For the sake of simplicity, we shall elect to use the extended mode, which specifies the operand by means of the two words immediately following the instruction. Therefore, memory location 0002 will contain the MSB of the operand address, while location 0003 will contain the LSB of the address. The operand in this case is the COUNTER located at address 0000. So, we can now fill in the Word column for the following addresses:

$0001 = 7F$ Operation code for CLR instruction.
$0002 = 00$ MSB of the address for COUNTER.
$0003 = 00$ LSB of the address for COUNTER.

The next instruction is located at memory location 0004. This is the LDAA instruction, which is to load a word from the A area into the accumulator. Here again, we will use the extended addressing mode to provide a 16-bit absolute memory address for the operand, to be located in the two words that immediately follow the instruction. First of all, we can fill in the operation code for the instruction, as found on the Instruction Set

Summary card. Memory location 0004 will therefore contain B6, the code for the extended mode LDAA instruction. The operand for this instruction will be a word in the A area. When this instruction is executed for the first time, it should cause the first word in the area to be loaded into the accumulator. From the memory map (Fig. 4-18), we can see that the first word of area A is located at memory address 0100 hexadecimal. Thus, we may now fill in the Word column for addresses 0004 through 0006 as follows:

0004 = B6   Operation code for LDAA instruction.
0005 = 01   MSB of address of first A area word.
0006 = 00   LSB of address of first A area word.

Step (3) is coded as follows. Now that the program has loaded a word from A area into the accumulator, the next step is to store it in the B area at the corresponding location. For this, we will use the STAA instruction, also in the extended addressing mode. The memory location 0007 will contain the operation code for the instruction, and the next two memory locations will contain the address of the operand. The operand in this case is to be the B area word in which the contents of the accumulator are to be stored. Referring again to the memory map, we see that the B area begins at memory location 0200, hexadecimal. From this and the Instruction Set Summary card, we can fill in the Word column for the following memory locations:

0007 = B7   Operation code for STAA instruction.
0008 = 02   MSB of address of first B area word.
0009 = 00   LSB of address of first B area word.

Since we are using the hexadecimal notation throughout this example, we observe that the next memory location is designated as 000A, the hexadecimal equivalent of ten. It is in this location that we shall find the next instruction in the program: from Step (4). Here, we are to increment the COUNTER, since we have just completed the moving of one word from the A area into the B area. For this, we shall use the INC instruction, also in the extended addressing mode. The operand in this case is the COUNTER, which is really located at memory address 0000. Now we can fill in the Word column for memory locations 000A through 000C as follows:

000A = 7C   Operation code for INC instruction.
000B = 00   MSB of the address of COUNTER.
000C = 00   LSB of the address of COUNTER.

The next step to be programmed is Step (5). Here, we must test the COUNTER to determine if arithmetic carry has occurred as a result of the foregoing INC instruction. This will be evidenced by the contents of COUNTER becoming zero as a result of the INC instruction, and the "zero" status flag in the CPU will be set. This allows us to use the BEQ (branch if equal to zero) instruction to accomplish the test. This instruction can be used only in the relative addressing mode, as observed from the Instruction Set Summary card. The displacement value that is to be arithmetically added to the PC register to produce the operand address is found in the word immediately following the instruction. The operand for this instruction consists of the address of the memory location to which the branch is to be made. This particular branch is to be made to the end of the program, designated as HALT. This is a WAI instruction that is located at memory address 0021.

Recall that the operation of "relative addressing mode" involves arithmetically adding a displacement value to the current value of the PC register, in order to obtain the actual address of the operand. It is important to note here that while any given instruction is being executed by the MC6800, the PC register actually contains the address of the *next* instruction in the program. Therefore, when calculating the displacement value the programmer must be aware of this fact. The PC register, at the time the branch is executed, contains the address of the BEQ instruction plus 2 since it is pointing to the next instruction in the program, the INC located at address 000F. (The BEQ remembers, is a two byte instruction.) To make the PC register contain the address of the WAI instruction located at 0021, we must add the displacement value, 12, hexadecimal. From this information we can fill in the Word column for memory addresses 000D and 000E as follows:

000D = 27   Operation code for BEQ instruction.
000E = 12   Displacement value to cause branch.

At this point, we must remember that if the "zero" status flag is not set at the time the BEQ instruction is executed, the program will not branch but instead will execute the next instruction, which is located at memory address 000F. Here we must increment the LSB of the A area address. This is, of course, the 16-bit address stored in the two words of memory immediately following the LDAA instruction. The first word contains the MSB of the address, while the second word contains the LSB of the address. Therefore, it is the word located at memory address 0006 that we must increment.

We will use the INC instruction in the extended addressing mode to accomplish the incrementing of the LSB of the A area address. This, like all extended mode instructions, will require three words of memory as follows:

000F = 7C   Operation code for INC instruction.
0010 = 00   MSB of location of LSB of A area address.
0011 = 06   LSB of location of LSB of A area address.

After incrementing the LSB of the A area address, the program must check to see if an arithmetic carry has occurred as a result of the increment operation. Again, if this has happened, the LSB of the address will have become zero, and the "zero" status flag inside the CPU will have been set. These conditions allow us to use the BNE instruction (branch if not equal to zero) to cause the program to branch around the instructions that will increment the MSB of the address (which need be done only if the carry has occurred). The instruction to which we will want to branch is at Step (9) and carries the label INCB. Here again, we will use the relative addressing mode to derive the actual memory address to which the branch is to be made. The current contents of the PC register are arithmetically added with the contents of the displacement word that immediately follows the instruction. Since the PC register contains the address of INC instruction 0014, and label INCB is located at memory address 0017, we must add the displacement 03 to the PC register to cause the branch. Therefore:

0012 = 26   Operation code for BNE instruction.
0013 = 03   Displacement value to cause branch.

However, if at this point the arithmetic carry has occurred as a result of incrementing the LSB of the A area address, we must also increment the MSB of the address. This is contained at memory location 0005. When the "zero" status flag in the CPU is set, the previous branch instruction will not be executed. Rather, the next instruction in the program will be executed. This will be another INC instruction, also in the extended addressing mode, which will increment the MSB of the A area address and require three words of memory.

0014 = 7C   Operation code for INC instruction.
0015 = 00   MSB of location of MSB of A area address.
0016 = 05   LSB of location of MSB of A area address.

At Step (9), then, we must begin to do the same thing to the B area address. This is, of course, the 16-bit address stored in the two words immediately following the STAA instruction at address 0007. Again, we will use the INC instruction in the extended addressing mode to accomplish the incrementing of the

B area address. This will require three words of memory as follows:

0017 = 7C   Operation code for INC instruction.
0018 = 00   MSB of location of LSB of B area address.
0019 = 09   LSB of location of LSB of B area address.

After the LSB of the B area address has been incremented, the program must check to see if there has been an arithmetic carry as a result of the execution of the INC instruction. This is done in the same manner as it was for the A area address; the BNE (branch if not equal to zero) instruction is used to cause a branch around the instructions for incrementing the MSB of the B area address. Here again, the BNE instruction is executed in the relative addressing mode. The PC register at this time will contain the address of the INC instruction, 001C. The location to which the branch is to be made is back at the beginning of the MOVE process. Since this is a branch "backwards," the displacement contained in the word immediately following the branch instruction must contain a negative value, in two's complement form. (See Appendix A for a development of this format.) Since the location to which the branch is to be made is memory address 0004, a displacement of negative 18 must be arithmetically added to the PC register. In two's complement notation, this is E8, hexadecimal. Therefore:

001A = 26   Operation code for BNE instruction.
001B = E8   Displacement value to cause branch.

Step (11) is the incrementing of the MSB of the B area address in the event that arithmetic carry occurred as a result of incrementing the LSB of the address. This is also accomplished through the use of the INC instruction and is executed only when the previous branch instruction was not executed. This is another extended addressing mode instruction, requiring three words of memory. The first contains the operation code, while the second and third contain the location of the B area address, which is actually the word immediately following the STAA instruction at memory address 0007. So, we fill in:

001C = 7C   Operation code for INC instruction.
001D = 00   MSB of location of MSB of B area address.
001E = 08   LSB of location of MSB of B area address.

Assuming that the MSB of the B area address required incrementing, the next instruction to be executed will be that contained at memory location 001F. Since the next thing we must do is to branch back to MOVE the next word from area A into area B, we will use the BRA (branch always) instruction.

This instruction will be executed in the relative addressing mode. Again, since the PC register contains the value 001F, and the MOVE label is located at address 0004, a negative displacement must be arithmetically added to cause the branch. That displacement value is negative 1B, which is E5 in two's complement notation. So, the next two words can be filled in:

001F = 20   Operation code for BRA instruction.
0020 = E5   Displacement value to cause branch.

Finally, at memory address 0021, we have the WAI instruction, which is branched to after all 256 words have been moved from area A into area B. This instruction requires only one word of memory and will cause the CPU to stop executing instructions. From the Instruction Set Summary card, we can fill in the Word column:

0021 = 3E   Operation code for WAI instruction.

Now we have finished hand-assembling the MOVE program. It has taken 0021 words hexadecimal, or 33 words decimal, to contain the complete program. We have traced the development of the program from the original, defined objective, through the initial sequential description, and on to the actual arrangement of the instructions. The two-digit hexadecimal numbers in the Word column are the actual "machine code" that must be stored in the memory at the specified addresses in order for the program to function.

Hand assembly of a program is obviously a very detailed process, even when only a small, simple program is concerned. If our aim is to program a computer to do some really complex task, hand assembly will probably not be practical. An "operating system" of some sort would have to be used, so that the programmer would not have to figure out the binary codes himself. One thing can be said in favor of the hand-assembly technique—it demands that the programmer fully understand the operation of the computer at the fundamental level. The programmer must know (or know where to find out) what the effects of processing each instruction will be, and must be able to use this knowledge to create a program that fulfills the processing objective. The beginner in microcomputer experimentation will undoubtedly write his first program using this approach. Methodically, the programmer will enter each instruction into its proper memory location via the front panel switches and lights. Once the program is loaded into memory, the programmer will pause for a moment, finger poised over the *start* switch, wondering if anything has been forgotten. If nothing has, the programmer will be rewarded with the satisfaction of a successful run.

NUMBERING SYSTEMS

"What's one and one and one and one and one and one and one and one and one and one?"
"I don't know," said Alice. "I lost count."
"She can't do addition," said the Red Queen.
(Lewis Carroll, *Through the Looking Glass*)

No one knows when the first number was recorded, but most likely it dates back to Biblical times. Among the oldest system of numbers was that of the Chinese, which was first based on a system of laying sticks in patterns and later was based on symbols drawn with pen and ink (Fig. A-1).

Calculating in these number systems was exceedingly difficult. This was because each time the basic numerals were exceeded, a new numeral had to be invented. In Roman numerals, when you needed to count above 100, you used a *C*, and above 1000 an *M*. The real problem came when these numbers had to be multiplied. The actual process of counting took place on counting boards, such as the Chinese abacus, where answers were converted back to the notation system.

Our current decimal system is much more streamlined than those of the ancient civilizations. We only have to learn the 10 basic symbols and the positional notation system in order to count to any number. For example, what is the meaning of the number 256? In positional notation, the value of each digit is determined by its position. The four in 4000 has a different value than the 4 in 400. Thus, in 256 we have three digits, and each must be "interpreted" in light of where it is in order and relation to the other digits. We learn that the rightmost digit is interpreted as the number of "ones," the next to the left as the number of "tens," and the next digit as "hundreds." The general formula for representing numbers in the decimal system using positional notation is:

$$a_1 10^{n-1} + a_2 10^{n-2} + \ldots + a_n$$

which is expressed as $a_1a_2a_3 \ldots a_n$, where n is the number of digits to the left of the decimal point. Therefore,

$$256 = (2 \times 10^2) + (5 \times 10^1) + (6 \times 10^0)$$
$$= 2 \text{ hundreds} + 5 \text{ tens} + 6 \text{ ones}$$

In the decimal system we use 10 as the basic multiplier. We call 10 the *base* or *radix*. Most of recorded history shows mankind counting in the decimal system (base 10). However, it is not difficult to imagine a race of one-armed people who used the quinary system (base 5). We see examples of the duodecimal system in clocks, rulers, the dozen, and so on.

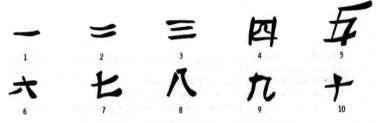

(A) Chinese "stick" number system.

(B) Chinese "pen-and-ink" number system.

Fig. A-1. First number systems.

THE BINARY SYSTEM

Although the seventeenth-century German mathematician Leibnitz was given most of the credit for invention of the binary number system with a base of 2, it was probably the ancient Chinese who realized the simple and natural way of representing numbers as powers of 2.

Early computers used relays and switches as their basic elements. The operation of a switch or a relay is itself binary in nature. A switch can either be on (1) or off (0). Modern computers use transistors like those found in televisions and radios. These components can be arranged to be in one or two "states": on or off. As a matter of fact, the more distinctly different the two states, the more reliable the computer's operation.

The idea is to make the devices work in such a manner that even slight changes in their characteristics will not affect the operation. The best way of doing this is to use a *bistable device*, which has two states.

If a bistable device is in stable state X, an energy pulse will drive it to state Y; and if the bistable component is in stable state Y, an energy pulse will drive it to state X. It is easy for a bistable component to represent the number 0 or 1:

stable state X = 1

stable state Y = 0

Counting

The same type of positional notation used in the decimal system is used in the binary. Since there are only two possible states for a numeral, either we count the position value or we don't count it. The general rule is: The binary number $a_1 a_2 a_3 \ldots a_n$ is expressed in decimal as:

$$a_1 2^{n-1} + a_2 2^{n-2} + \ldots + a_n$$

Therefore, the binary number 11010 is converted to decimal as follows:

$$N = a_1 2^{5-1} + a_2 2^{4-1} + a_3 2^{3-1} + a_4 2^{2-1} + a_5 2^{1-1}$$
$$= a_1 16 + a_2 8 + a_3 4 + a_4 2 + a_5 1$$

Substituting the values for a_1, a_2, a_3, a_4, and a_5:

$$11010 = (1 \times 16) + (1 \times 8) + (0 \times 4) + (1 \times 2) + (0 \times 1)$$
$$= 16 + 8 + 0 + 2 + 0$$
$$= 26 \text{ (decimal system)}$$

Table A-1 lists the first 20 binary numbers.

Table A-1. The First 20 Binary Numbers

Decimal	Binary	Decimal	Binary
1	1	11	1011
2	10	12	1100
3	11	13	1101
4	100	14	1110
5	101	15	1111
6	110	16	10000
7	111	17	10001
8	1000	18	10010
9	1001	19	10011
10	1010	20	10100

A simpler way to convert binary numbers to decimal is to use a weighting table (Fig. A-2). This is simply a reduction of the expansion formula just presented. Write down the value of the positions in the binary number over the binary digits, arrange them as an addition, and add them.

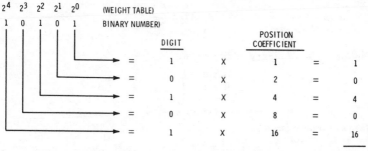

Fig. A-2. Binary-to-decimal conversion using the weighting method.

Frequently we will want to convert in the opposite direction, from decimal to binary. For this method we repeatedly divide the decimal number by 2, and the remainder after each division is used to indicate the coefficients of the binary number to be formed. Fig. A-3 shows the conversion of 47_{10} to binary. Note that decimal 47 is written 47_{10} and that binary numbers are given the subscript 2 if there is danger of confusing the number systems.

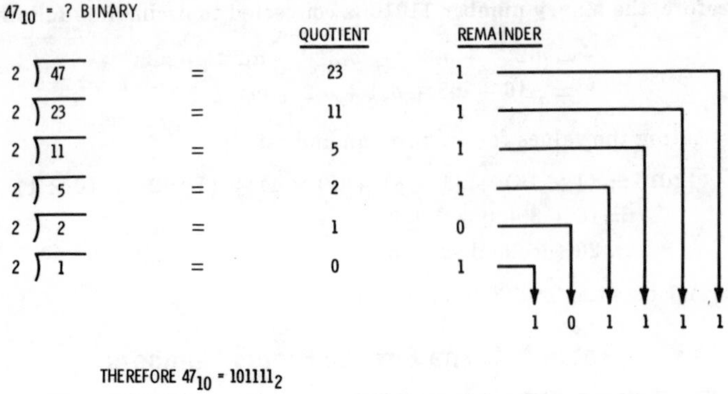

47_{10} = ? BINARY

THEREFORE $47_{10} = 101111_2$

Fig. A-3. Decimal-to-binary conversion using the division method.

Fractional numbers are treated in the same manner as in the decimal system. In the decimal system:

$$0.128 = (1 \times 10^{-1}) + (2 \times 10^{-2}) + (8 \times 10^{-3})$$

In the binary system:

$$0.101 = (1 \times 2^{-1}) + (0 \times 2^{-2}) + (1 \times 2^{-3})$$

Binary Addition and Subtraction

Addition in binary is as easy as addition in decimal, and follows the same rules. In adding decimal $1 + 8$, we get a sum of 9. This is the highest-value digit. Adding 1 to 9 requires that we change the digit back to 0 *and carry 1*. Similarly, adding binary $0 + 1$, we reach the highest-value binary digit, 1. Adding 1 to 1 requires that we change the 1 back to a 0 and carry 1, i.e., $1 + 1 = 10$. Thus, for example, add binary 101 to 111:

$$
\begin{array}{ll}
101_2 = & 5_{10} \\
+\ 111_2 = & 7_{10} \\
\hline
1100_2 = & 12_{10}
\end{array}
$$

The four rules of binary addition are:

$$
\begin{array}{l}
0 + 0 = 0 \\
0 + 1 = 1 \\
1 + 0 = 1 \\
1 + 1 = 0,\ \text{carry 1}
\end{array}
$$

Here are some examples:

101	5	11.01	$3\frac{1}{4}$
+ 110	6	101.11	$5\frac{3}{4}$
1011	11	1001.00	9

Subtraction is just inverted addition. It is necessary to establish a convention for subtracting a large digit from a small digit. This condition occurs in binary math when we subtract a 1 from a 0. The remainder is 1, and we borrow 1 from the column to the left. Just as in decimal subtraction, if the digit on the left is a 1, we make it a zero, and if it's a zero, we make it a 1. The rules for binary subtraction are:

$$0 - 0 = 0$$
$$1 - 0 = 1$$
$$1 - 1 = 0$$
$$0 - 1 = 1, \text{ borrow } 1$$

Here are two examples:

	10000	16	110.01	6¼
−	11	− 3	−100.1	−4½
	1101	13	1.11	1¾

Binary Multiplication and Division

There are only four basic multiplications to remember in the binary system, instead of the usual 100 we memorize in the decimal system. The binary multiplication table is:

$$0 \times 0 = 0$$
$$1 \times 0 = 0$$
$$0 \times 1 = 0$$
$$1 \times 1 = 1$$

The following examples illustrate how easy binary multiplication is compared with decimal. The rule to remember is: "copy the multiplicand if the multiplier is a 1, and copy all 0's if the multiplier is a 0. Then add down, as in decimal multiplication."

Binary	*Decimal*	*Binary*	*Decimal*
1100	12	1.01	1.25
×1010	×10	×10.1	×2.5
0000	120	101	625
1100		1010	250
0000		11.001	3.125
1100			
1111000			

Binary division is also very simple. Division by zero is forbidden (meaningless), just as in decimal division. The binary division table is:

$$\frac{0}{1} = 0$$

$$\frac{1}{1} = 1$$

Examples of binary division are:

Binary	*Decimal*
101	5
101)11001	5)25
101	
101	
101	

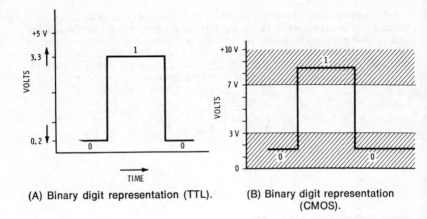

(A) Binary digit representation (TTL).

(B) Binary digit representation (CMOS).

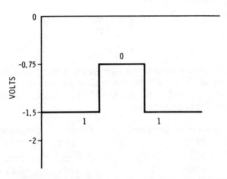

(C) Binary digit representation—negative logic (ECL).

Fig. A-4. Representing binary numbers.

Because of the difficult binary additions and subtractions that result when the numbers are large, octal or hexadecimal notation is often used.

Representing Binary Numbers

Information in digital computers of today is processed by the switching and storing of electrical signals. Computers operating in the binary number system need represent only one of two values (1 and 0) at a time. A single wire can be utilized for this purpose. A method for representing a binary digit on a signal line is shown in Fig. A-4A. In this method a small positive voltage is used to represent a 0, and a larger positive dc voltage is used to represent a 1.

Much importance is placed on the actual voltage values used to represent the binary digit. Usually, the circuitry used to transmit and receive these signals determines the range of voltages. The most ideal circuit is one in which the two logic levels are far apart (Fig. A-4B).

Note that the "1" signal is positive with respect to the "0" signal. This convention could also have been reversed, i.e., the negativemost signal

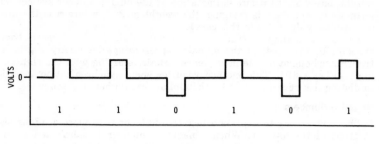

(A) RZ method of representing binary digits.

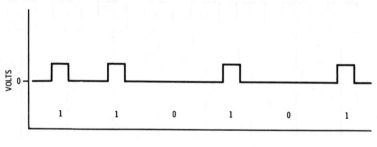

(B) NRZ method of representing binary digits.

Fig. A-5. Pulse representation of binary numbers.

called a "1" and the more positive signal a "0." (See Fig. A-4C.) Usually, one convention is chosen by the designer and then used throughout the computer.

Pulse Representation of Binary Numbers

Binary digits are often transmitted and received as a burst of pulses. Fig. A-5A shows a system in which a positive pulse represents a 1 and a negative pulse a 0. The signal line remains at some in-between value when no pulse is being sent. This technique is used frequently in magnetic recording, and is called *return-to-zero* (RZ) encoding.

A more popular technique is shown in Fig. A-6B. A 1 is represented by a pulse, and a 0 as no pulse. The receive circuitry must keep in synchronization with the incoming signal in order to know when a binary digit is occurring. This technique is called *non-return-to-zero* (NRZ) encoding.

Serial and Parallel Transmission

So far, methods of representing and transmitting a single binary digit have been illustrated. We will find that it is often necessary to transmit complete binary numbers, which is accomplished by transmitting each binary digit over its own wire. Thus, an n-digit binary number would require n wires or signal lines. This is called *parallel transmission*. Fig. A-6A illustrates an 8-bit binary number (10010101) being transmitted over eight parallel lines. In such a system each line is assigned a different weight, based on the positional notation of the binary number system. The leftmost binary digit is assigned the weight of 2^{n-1}, where n is the number of binary digits (8 in this case).

The other method of transmitting binary data is called *serial transmission*. In this method the signals representing the binary digits are transmitted one at a time in sequence, usually starting with the rightmost digit (Fig. A-6B). This method requires some synchronization in order to distinguish several 0's or 1's that follow each other in a sequence.

Negative Numbers

The normal way to express a negative number is to place a minus sign in front of the number. When a negative number is subtracted from a positive number, we *change the sign and add*. For example, $256 - (-128) = 256 + 128 = 384$.

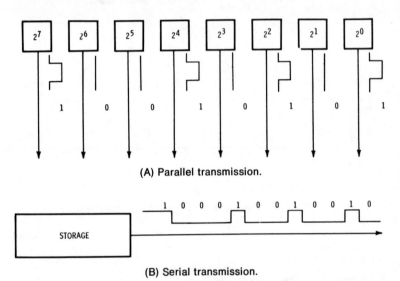

(A) Parallel transmission.

(B) Serial transmission.

Fig. A-6. Parallel and serial transmission.

Digital computers use binary storage devices to store and represent binary digits. Seven such devices can represent the binary numbers from 0000000 to 1111111 (0 to 127_{10}). However, if we wish to increase the range to include the negative numbers from 0000000 to -1111111, we need another binary digit, or bit. This bit is called the *sign bit* and is placed in front of the most significant digit of the binary number.

The convention for the sign bit is: If the sign bit is 0, the number is positive; and if the sign bit is a 1, the number is negative. The remaining digits form the absolute value of the number. This numerical storage mode is called *signed binary*. Fig. A-7A shows signed binary numbers from $+127$ to -127, and the signed binary number line is shown in Fig. A-7B.

Signed binary, although frequently used, has a few minor flaws that make it less flexible than other codes for negative numbers. Any arithmetic operation requires checking the sign bit and then either adding or subtracting the numerical values, based on the signs.

INTEGER	SIGNED BINARY CODE							
	s	b_7	b_6	b_5	b_4	b_3	b_2	b_1
+127	0	1	1	1	1	1	1	1
+126	0	1	1	1	1	1	1	0
↓								
↓								
↓								
+3	0	0	0	0	0	0	1	1
+2	0	0	0	0	0	0	1	0
+1	0	0	0	0	0	0	0	1
0	0	0	0	0	0	0	0	0
−1	1	0	0	0	0	0	0	1
−2	1	0	0	0	0	0	1	0
−3	1	0	0	0	0	0	1	1
↑								
↑								
↑								
−126	1	1	1	1	1	1	1	0
−127	1	1	1	1	1	1	1	1

(A) Seven-bit–magnitude table.

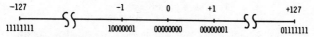

(B) Signed binary number line (seven-bit magnitude).

Fig. A-7. Signed binary code.

The Use of Complements

The use of complemented binary numbers makes it possible to add or subtract binary numbers using only circuitry for addition. To see how negative numbers are used in the computer, consider a mechanical register, such as a car mileage indicator, being rotated backwards. A five-digit register approaching and passing through zero would read as follows:

```
00005
00004
00003
00002
00001
00000
99999
99998
99997
etc.
```

It should be clear that the number 99998 corresponds to −2. Furthermore, if we add

$$
\begin{array}{r}
00005 \\
+\ \underline{99998} \\
1\ \ 00003
\end{array}
$$

and ignore the carry to the left, we have effectively formed the operation of subtraction: $5 - 2 = 3$.

The number 99998 is called the *ten's complement* of 2. The ten's complement of any decimal number may be formed by subtracting each digit of the number from 9, and then adding 1 to the least significant digit of the number formed. For example:

normal   *ten's complement*
subtraction   *subtraction*

$$
\begin{array}{cc}
\begin{array}{r}
89 \\
-\ \underline{23} \\
66
\end{array}
&
\begin{array}{rr}
89 & 89 \\
-\ \underline{23} & +\ \underline{77} \\
& 1\ \ 66 \\
& \text{DROP CARRY}
\end{array}
\end{array}
$$

Two's Complement

The two's complement is the binary equivalent of the ten's complement in the decimal system. It is defined as that number which, when added to the original number, will result in a sum of zero, ignoring the carry. The following example points this out:

$$
\begin{array}{ll}
\begin{array}{r}
1101 \\
\underline{0011} \\
1\ \ 0000
\end{array}
&
\begin{array}{l}
\text{number} \\
\text{two's complement} \\
\text{sum}
\end{array}
\end{array}
$$

IGNORE CARRY

The easiest method of finding the two's complement of a binary number is to first find the one's complement, which is formed by setting each bit to the opposite value:

$$
\begin{array}{ll}
11011101 & \text{number} \\
00100010 & \text{one's complement}
\end{array}
$$

The two's complement of the number is then obtained by adding 1 to the least significant digit of the one's complement:

$$
\begin{array}{ll}
11011101 & \text{number} \\
00100010 & \text{one's complement} \\
\underline{+1} & \text{add one} \\
00100011 & \text{two's complement}
\end{array}
$$

The complete signed two's complement code is obtained for negative numbers by using a 1 for the sign bit, and two's complement for the magnitude of the number. Fig. A-8A shows the signed two's complement code, and its number line is shown in Fig. A-8B.

In contrast to the signed binary code, in the signed two's complement code, numbers can be added without regard to their signs and the result will always be correct. The following examples should make this clear:

$$
\begin{array}{lll}
\begin{array}{rr}
0000101 & 5 \\
+\underline{1111110} & +\ (-2) \\
1\ \ 0000011 & 3
\end{array}
&
\begin{array}{rr}
1111011 & -5 \\
+\underline{0000010} & +\ (+2) \\
11111101 & (-3)
\end{array}
&
\begin{array}{rr}
1111011 & -5 \\
+\underline{1111110} & +\ (-2) \\
1\ \ 1111001 & (-7)
\end{array}
\end{array}
$$

IGNORE   IGNORE

INTEGER	CODE SIGNED 2's COMPLEMENT							
	s	b_7	b_6	b_5	b_4	b_3	b_2	b_1
+127	0	1	1	1	1	1	1	1
+126	0	1	1	1	1	1	1	0
┊				┊				
┊				┊				
┊				┊				
+3	0	0	0	0	0	0	1	1
+2	0	0	0	0	0	0	1	0
+1	0	0	0	0	0	0	0	1
0	0	0	0	0	0	0	0	0
−1	1	1	1	1	1	1	1	1
−2	1	1	1	1	1	1	1	0
−3	1	1	1	1	1	1	0	1
┊				┊				
┊				┊				
┊				┊				
−126	1	0	0	0	0	0	1	0
−127	1	0	0	0	0	0	0	1
−128	1	0	0	0	0	0	0	0

(A) Seven-bit–magnitude table.

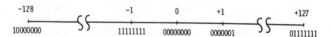

(B) Two's complement number line.

Fig. A-8. Signed two's complement code.

Notice that it is impossible to add +64 to +64 in a 7-bit code and +128 to +128 in an 8-bit code. Also note that in comparing the two systems, signed binary and two's complement, the largest negative two's complement number that can be represented in 8 bits is −128, while in signed binary it's −127. Changing a negative integer from signed binary to two's complement requires simply complementing all bits except the sign bit, and adding 1.

Binary-Coded Number Representation

Since computers operate in the binary number system, while people use the decimal system, it was only natural that some intermediate system be developed. Computers, and some calculators and "intelligent" instruments, use a *binary-coded decimal* system. In such systems, a group of binary bits is used to represent each of the 10 decimal digits.

The binary-coded decimal (bcd) system is called a "weighted binary code" with the weights 8, 4, 2, and 1, as shown in Table A-2. Notice that 4 binary bits are required for each decimal digit, and that each digit is assigned a weight: the leftmost bit has a weight of 8; the rightmost bit a weight of 1.

There's a slight problem with using 4 bits to represent 10 decimal values. Since $2^4 = 16$, the 4 bits could actually represent 16 values. However, the next choice down, 3 bits, allows only 2^3, or 8, possible digits, which is insufficient. To represent the decimal number 127 in bcd, 12 binary bits are required instead of seven if we use pure binary:

$$
\begin{array}{ccc}
1 & 2 & 7 \\
0001 & 0010 & 0111
\end{array}
$$

The bcd system has another property that makes it less flexible for binary computation in the computer. The difficulty lies in forming complements of its numbers. As was pointed out, it is common practice to perform subtraction by complementing the subtrahend and adding 1. When the bcd 8-4-2-1 system is used, the complement formed by inverting all the bits may produce an illegal bcd digit. For example, complementing the bcd number 0010 (2_{10}) gives 1101 (13_{10}), which is not a bcd code.

To solve this problem, several other codes have been developed. For example, the *excess-three code* is formed by adding 3 to the decimal number and then forming the bcd code. For example:

$$
\begin{array}{rl}
4 & \text{number} \\
\underline{+3} & \text{add for excess-three} \\
7 &
\end{array}
$$

$$7 = 0111 \quad \text{convert 7 to bcd}$$

Table A-2 also shows the excess-three codes for the 10 decimal digits. Now the complement of the excess-three code doesn't form any illegal bcd digits, i.e., 10_{10} or above.

Table A-2. Binary-Coded Number Representation

Decimal Digit	Binary-Coded Decimal	Excess-3 Coded Binary	2-4-2-1 Coded Binary			
			Weight of Bit			
			2	4	2	1
0	0000	0011	0	0	0	0
1	0001	0100	0	0	0	1
2	0010	0101	0	0	1	0
3	0011	0110	0	0	1	1
4	0100	0111	0	1	0	0
5	0101	1000	1	0	1	1
6	0110	1001	1	1	0	0
7	0111	1010	1	1	0	1
8	1000	1011	1	1	1	0
9	1001	1100	1	1	1	1

The excess-three code is not a weighted code, since the sum of the bits does not equal the number being represented. On the other hand, the bcd 8-4-2-1 code is weighted but forms illegal complements.

A weighted code that does form legal complements is the *2-4-2-1 code* in Table A-2.

OCTAL NUMBER SYSTEM

It is probably quite evident by now that the binary number system, although nice for computers, is a little cumbersome for human usage. For example, communicating binary 11011010 over a telephone would be "one-one-zero-one-one-zero-one-zero," which is quite a mouthful. Also, it is easy to make errors when adding and subtracting large binary numbers. The octal (base 8) number system alleviates most of these problems and is frequently used in the microcomputer literature.

The octal system uses the digits 0 through 7 in forming numbers. Table A-3 shows octal numbers and their decimal equivalents.

Table A-3. First 13 Octal Digits

Decimal	Octal	Binary	Decimal	Octal	Binary
0	0	0	7	7	111
1	1	1	8	10	1000
2	2	10	9	11	1001
3	3	11	10	12	1010
4	4	100	11	13	1011
5	5	101	12	14	1100
6	6	110	13	15	1101

Octal numbers are converted to decimal numbers by using the same expansion formula as that used in binary-to-decimal conversion, except that 8 is used for the base instead of 2.

$$\begin{aligned}
(\text{octal}) \ 167 &= (1 \times 8^2) + (6 \times 8^1) + (7 \times 8^0) \\
&= (1 \times 64) + (6 \times 8) + (7 \times 1) \\
&= \quad 64 \quad + \quad 48 \quad + \quad 7 \\
&= 119 \ (\text{decimal})
\end{aligned}$$

A *weighting table* (Fig. A-9) is a quick way to convert octal values to decimal.

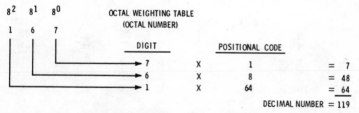

Fig. A-9. Octal-to-decimal conversion.

The primary use of octal is as a convenient way of recording values stored in binary registers. This is accomplished by using a grouping method to convert the binary value to its octal equivalent. The binary number is grouped by threes, starting with the bit corresponding to $2^0 = 1$ and grouping to the left of it. Then each binary group is converted to its octal equivalent. For example, convert 11110101 to octal:

```
    011  110  101   binary number
     3    6    5    octal equivalent
  implied 0
```

The largest 8-bit octal number is 377_8, and the largest 7-bit octal number is 177_8. Negative octal numbers in 8-bit signed two's complement cover 377_8 (-1_{10}) to 200_8 (-128_{10}).

Conversion from decimal to octal is performed by repeated division by 8 and using the remainder as a digit in the octal number being formed. Fig. A-10 illustrates this method.

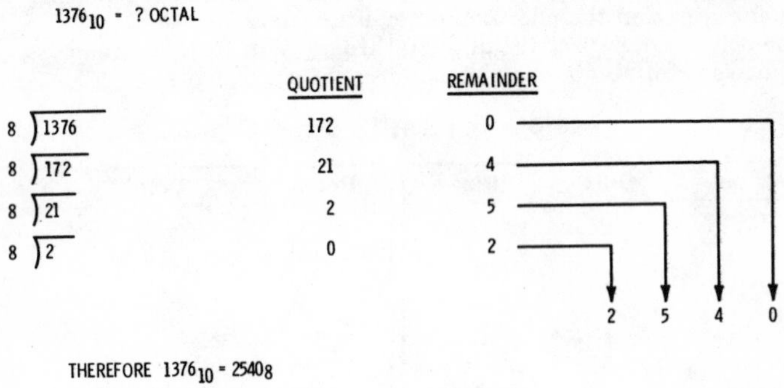

Fig. A-10. Decimal-to-octal conversion.

Addition in Octal

Octal addition is easy if we remember the following rules (which we will find also apply to hexadecimal):

1. If the sum of any column is equal to or greater than the base of the system being used, the base must be subtracted from the sum to obtain the final result of the column.
2. If the sum of any column is equal to or greater than the base, there will be a carry, equal to the number of times the base was subtracted.
3. If the result of any column is less than the base, the base is not subtracted and no carry will be generated.

Examples:

octal	decimal		octal		decimal
5	= 5		35	=	29
+3	= 3		+63	=	+51
8			1 10 8		
−8			−8 −8		
10	= 8		1 2 0	=	80

Octal Subtraction

Octal subtraction can be performed directly or in the complemented mode by using addition. In direct subtraction, whenever a borrow is needed, an 8 is borrowed and added to the number. For example:

$$2022_8 - 1234_8 = ?$$

$$\begin{array}{r} 2022_8 \\ 1234_8 \\ \hline 566_8 \end{array}$$

Octal subtraction may also be performed by finding the eight's complement and adding. The eight's complement is found by adding 1 to the seven's complement. The seven's complement of the number may be found by subtracting each digit from 7. For example:

$$377_8 - 261_8 = ?$$

a)
$$
\begin{array}{r}
777 \\
-261 \\
\hline
516 \\
+1 \\
\hline
517 \\
\end{array}
$$
    (second number)

516   7's complement

517   8's complement

b)
$$
\begin{array}{r}
377 \\
+517 \\
\hline
\end{array}
$$
   (first number)

   8's complement of 261

$$
\begin{array}{rrr}
9 & 9 & 14 \\
-8 & -8 & -8 \\
\hline
1 & 1 & 6 \\
\end{array} = 116_8
$$

Octal Multiplication

Octal multiplication is performed by using an octal multiplication table (see Table A-4) in the same manner as a decimal table would be used. All additions are done by using the rules for octal addition. For example:

$$17_8 \times 6_8 = ?$$

octal		decimal
17	=	15
×6	=	×6
		90

$$
\begin{array}{rrr}
1 & 11 & 2 \\
-0 & -8 & -0 \\
\hline
1 & 3 & 2 \\
\end{array} = 132_8
$$

$$177_8 \times 27_8 = ?$$

octal		decimal
177	=	127
×27	=	×23
1371		381
376		254
		2921

$$
\begin{array}{rrrr}
5 & 11 & 13 & 1 \\
-0 & -8 & -8 & -0 \\
\hline
5 & 3 & 5 & 1 \\
\end{array} = 5351_8
$$

Numbers are multiplied by looking up the result in the table. The result of any product larger than 7 (the radix or base) is carried and then octally added to the next product. The results are then summed up by using octal addition.

Table A-4. Octal Multiplication Table

×	0	1	2	3	4	5	6	7
0	0	0	0	0	0	0	0	0
1	0	1	2	3	4	5	6	7
2	0	2	4	6	10	12	14	16
3	0	3	6	11	14	17	22	25
4	0	4	10	14	20	24	30	34
5	0	5	12	17	24	31	36	43
6	0	6	14	22	30	36	44	52
7	0	7	16	25	34	43	52	61

Octal Division

Octal division uses the same principles as decimal division. All multiplication and subtraction involved, however, must be done in octal. Refer to the octal multiplication table. Some examples:

$$144_8 \div 2_8 = ?$$

$$\frac{144_8}{2_8} = \frac{100_{10}}{2_{10}} = 50_{10} = 62_8$$

$$62_8 \div 2_8 = ?$$

$$1714_8 \div 22_8 = ?$$

$$31 = 31_8 = 25_{10}$$

$$\begin{array}{r} 31 \\ 2\overline{)62} \\ 6 \\ \hline 02 \\ 2 \\ \hline 0 \end{array}$$

$$66 = 66_8 = 54_{10}$$

$$\begin{array}{r} 66 \\ 22\overline{)1714} \\ 154 \\ \hline 154 \\ 154 \\ \hline \end{array}$$

THE HEXADECIMAL SYSTEM

Hexadecimal is another important and often-used computer number system. "Hex" uses the radix 16 and therefore has 16 digits. The first 10 digits are represented by the decimal digits 0 through 9, and the remaining six are indicated by the letters A, B, C, D, E, and F. There is nothing special about these letters, and any other letters could have been used. Table A-5 shows the first 16 hexadecimal digits.

Table A-5. First 16 Hexadecimal Digits

Binary	Hexadecimal	Decimal
0000	0	0
0001	1	1
0010	2	2
0011	3	3
0100	4	4
0101	5	5
0110	6	6
0111	7	7
1000	8	8
1001	9	9
1010	A	10
1011	B	11
1100	C	12
1101	D	13
1110	E	14
1111	F	15

Binary numbers are easily converted to hex by grouping the bits in groups of four, starting on the right, converting the results to decimal, and then converting to hex. For example:

$$\begin{array}{llll} 1000 & 1010 & 1101 & \text{binary} \\ 8 & 10 & 13 & \text{decimal} \\ 8 & A & D & \text{hex} = 8AD_{16} \end{array}$$

As you can probably tell, hex is preferred over octal whenever the binary number to be represented is 16 bits or more. This is because the hex code is more compact than the octal equivalent.

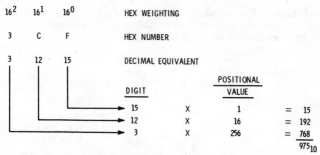

Fig. A-11. Hexadecimal-to-decimal conversion.

Conversion from hexadecimal to decimal is straightforward but time-consuming. The expansion formula, or a weighting table with an intermediary hex-to-decimal conversion, is used as shown in Fig. A-11.

Conversion from decimal to hex is performed by repeatedly dividing by 16, and converting the remainder to a hex digit. The quotient becomes the next number to divide. This is shown in Fig. A-12.

$$975 = ?_{16}$$

	QUOTIENT	REMAINDER IN DECIMAL	REMAINDER IN HEX
975/16	60	15	F
60/16	3	12	C
3/16	0	3	3

3 C F

Fig. A-12. Decimal-to-hexadecimal conversion.

Hexadecimal Addition

Addition in hex is similar to the addition procedure for octal, except the hex digits are first converted to decimal. For example:

```
      3CF + 2AD = ?
  +  2AD = +2   10   13
     3CF =   3   12   15
           ─────────────
             6   23   28
           -0 -16  -16
           ─────────────
             6    7   12 = 67C
```

Subtraction in Hexadecimal

Subtraction in hex may be accomplished by either the direct or the complement method. In the direct method, the hex digits are converted to decimal. If a borrow is required, 16 is added to the desired number and the digit borrowed from is decreased by 1. In the complement method, the sixteen's complement of the subtrahend is determined and the two num-

197

bers are added. The sixteen's complement is found by adding 1 to the fifteen's complement. The fifteen's complement is found by subtracting each of the hex digits from F. For example:

```
                    2BD − 1CE = ?
        FFF =      15   15   15
        −1CE      − 1   12   14        second number
                  ─────────────
                   14    3    1        15's complement
                             + 1
                  ─────────────
                   14    3    2        16's complement
        2BD =     + 2   11   13        first number
                ┌──────────────
              1   16   14   15
                 −16   −0   −0
                  ─────────────
   └─ignore carry   0   14   15     = EF (answer)
```

Hexadecimal Multiplication

Direct hex multiplication is rather tedious and time-consuming. This is because there are 256 entries in a hex multiplication table. The best method is to convert to decimal by using the expansion polynomial and then convert back from decimal to hex after computation.

MEMORIES

This appendix classifies memories as read/write and read-only types. Several examples of each type are given.

READ/WRITE MEMORIES

Read/write memories are memories in which the stored information is available at any time and can be changed during normal operation of the system. Bipolar memories, static and dynamic MOS memories, as well as CMOS and SOS cells, are of this type.

Bipolar Memory

The simple bipolar-transistor cell is made of bipolar npn transistors in a cross-coupled configuration, as shown in Fig. B-1. Two emitters are diffused into the memory-cell transistors to permit connection of the cell to read and write circuits.

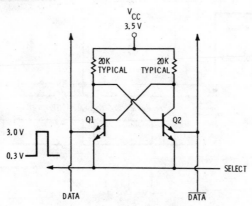

Fig. B-1. Bipolar (TTL) storage cell.

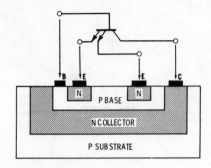

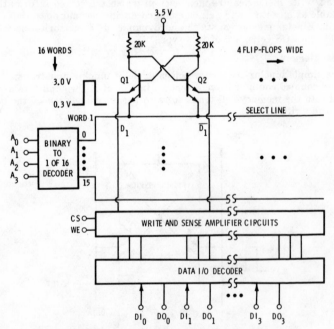

Fig. B-2. Dual-emitter npn transistor schematic symbol and physical cross section.

Fig. B-2 shows the basic bipolar cell building block: a two-emitter npn transistor. Either one of the two emitters is capable of conducting base-emitter current. When conducting, either emitter will turn the transistor on. To operate the transistor, a biasing voltage, positive with respect to the voltage to be used on the emitters, is provided by pull-up resistors. A negative-going voltage on either emitter will then turn the device on.

Fig. B-3 shows how two dual-emitter transistors are biased and cross-coupled to form a memory cell in a 16-by-4 bipolar RAM. In the normal nonaccessed state, the DATA and $\overline{\text{DATA}}$ (D and $\overline{\text{D}}$) lines are held at a positive potential so that they are nonconducting. In this state, the cell simply stores a 1 or a 0. If Q_1 is turned on, it shorts out the biasing resistor for Q_2; thus, Q_2 is off and the biasing resistor for Q_1 is not shorted. This is the state for storing 1. For storing 0, Q_2 is on and Q_1 is off.

Fig. B-3. Sixty-four–bit bipolar RAM organized 16 by 4.

The SELECT line is normally biased at about 0.3 volt to allow the cell to retain its data. To read data from this cell, the SELECT line is brought high to about 3 volts. A differential amplifier (not shown) connected to the DATA and $\overline{\text{DATA}}$ lines senses the state of the cell. If Q_1 is on, the DATA line will be more positive than the $\overline{\text{DATA}}$ line, indicating 1. If Q_2 is on, the $\overline{\text{DATA}}$ line will be more positive than the DATA line, indicating a 0 is stored in the cell. Many cells can share the same DATA and $\overline{\text{DATA}}$ lines with one common differential amplifier attached. In this configuration, only one cell is selected at a time by placing a positive voltage on its SELECT line. The other cells are not affected by the DATA and $\overline{\text{DATA}}$ lines, as their SELECT lines are at a lower potential (0.3 V).

Writing is similar to reading, in that the cell to be affected is selected by applying a positive voltage to the SELECT line. To write a 0, the cell selected, then the $\overline{\text{DATA}}$ line is brought low to about 2 volts. This turns Q_2 on. Transistor Q_2, being on, shorts the base-bias resistor to Q_1, turning Q_1 off. After writing, the $\overline{\text{DATA}}$ line is returned to its 0.3-V normal state. Writing a 1 is the same, except that the DATA line, rather than the $\overline{\text{DATA}}$ line, is brought low.

Bipolar cells commonly use two types of npn transistor technologies. Regular npn's are used for medium- and low-speed memories. Schottky-clamped npn's are used to make ultrafast-access bipolar memories. In both cases, cell configurations are essentially the same.

Typical standby power for the bipolar cell is about 800 microwatts. Read current is about 150 microamperes; delay is on the order of 20 nanoseconds for the Schottky bipolar memory.

Static MOS Memory

Although bipolar memory cells are high-speed devices, and are well understood, they have quite a few drawbacks when used as dense-memory ICs. The biggest drawback is that bipolar cells use large amount of power to keep the "on" transistor on, and this limits the maximum attainable density. MOS (Metal-Oxide Semiconductor) transistors are by far the transistors most often used for memory ICs, and they continue to be improved each year.

While bipolar transistors require two types of current carriers—holes and electrons—MOS devices require only one major current carrier, namely electrons for n channel, and holes for p channel. They are called *unipolar* for this reason.

There are two possible modes of operation of MOS devices: the enhancement mode and the depletion mode. Early MOS technology was depletion mode only, which uses a physical channel diffused in the production process. Later, enhancement mode caught on. These enhancement-mode devices simply induce the electronic equivalent of a channel, further simplifying the MOS device. Enhancement is by far the most commonly used mode of operation for memories.

A primary distinction between MOS and bipolar arises from the fact that bipolar transistors are "bulk" devices. The active region of recombination lies quite a distance from the base surface. MOS devices, on the other hand, utilize a surface effect, which takes place at the insulator interface. These factors add up to make a MOS transistor three-terminal solid-state device that requires almost no input current to operate, quite in contrast to the current-operated bipolar device. MOS input impedance is on the order of 10^{14} ohms.

A final reason for the dominance of MOS in memory is that it inherently uses up less area on the silicon chip, a major cost factor in high-

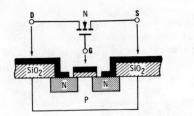

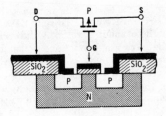

N & P = N DOPED AND P DOPED SILICON (Si)

(A) NMOS inverter schematic symbol and cross section.

(B) PMOS inverter schematic symbol and cross section.

Fig. B-4. MOS transistors.

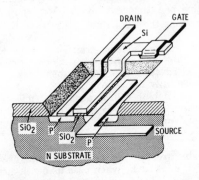

Fig. B-5. PMOS inverter physical layout.

density chips. Furthermore, the MOS transistor can act like a high-value resistor on the chip by tying its drain to the gate. This eliminates the need to diffuse separate resistors on the chip. Values greater than 10^4 ohms result due to the constant-current–source mode of MOS operation.

The fabrication of MOS can be either p channel or n channel. For sheer speed, NMOS is the choice, as the mobility of electrons (the primary current carrier) is three to four times that of the holes in the PMOS. This

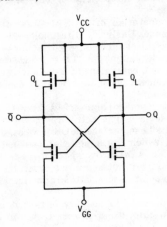

Fig. B-6. Simplest type of MOS storage element.

means three to four times reduction in area for equivalent performance. NMOS is unfortunately harder to make than PMOS. Fig. B-4 illustrates the schematic and cross section for n- and p-channel MOS transistors.

Fig. B-5 shows the actual physical structure of a p-channel MOS inverter. As we can see, the transistor is composed mostly of a silicon dioxide layer, deposited on an n substrate, with a large well occurring where the drain, gate, and source are formed. The channel is made of p-type holes, moving between the drain and source, with the voltage on the gate controlling the movement.

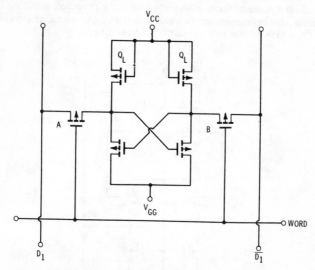

Fig. B-7. Six-transistor PMOS storage element with sense transmission gates A and B.

There are a number of ways to make a MOS memory cell using MOS transistors. Fig. B-6 shows the simplest type of MOS storage element. Here the inverters are cross coupled, as in the bipolar cell, to form a simple flip-flop. Instead of depositing or diffusing separate resistors for drain loads as in the bipolar cell, two additional MOS transistors, Q_L, are diffused as constant-current loads. By connecting the MOS gate to the drain, the device acts like a high-value current source and hence a high-value resistor taking up very little space.

The actual implementation of the MOS storage element is demonstrated in Fig. B-7. This is a PMOS six-transistor cell with six interconnects. The number of interconnects tells us how many connections must be made to each storage element to use it as a memory. Obviously, the smaller that this number of interconnects can be made, the less costly the final IC will be. To read data from the cell (i.e., to determine the state of the flip-flop), the WORD line is raised and the data lines (D_1 and $\overline{D_1}$) are sensed. This means that the state is output to an external circuit. To write data into the cell, the WORD line is raised, turning on A and B gates, and the appropriate data line (D_1 or $\overline{D_1}$) is forced to change state. This will in turn cause the flip-flop to change to the desired state.

NMOS cells, on the other hand, differ in complexity from the PMOS structure. The tradeoff is usually speed for a higher power dissipation.

The cell in Fig. B-8 is an eight-transistor static cell, used in the Signetics 2602 static 1024 × 1 RAM. Transistors Q_1 and Q_2 provide pull-up current for the static flip-flop consisting of Q_3 and Q_4. Transistors Q_5/Q_7 and Q_6/Q_8 are two transmission gates connecting the cell to true and inverted data bus lines shared with other cells. When both X and Y select lines are at logic 1, the transmission gates open (conduct). To write a logic 1, the write circuit (not shown) places logic 1 on the DATA line and logic 0 on the $\overline{\text{DATA}}$ line, and then selects the cell by bringing both the X and Y select lines for that cell to logic 1. This sets the cell to Q4 on and Q3 off. Writing a logic 0 is the same process with DATA and $\overline{\text{DATA}}$ reversed. Reading is done by opening the transmission gates and sensing the DATA and $\overline{\text{DATA}}$ logic levels. The state of the cell appears on these lines.

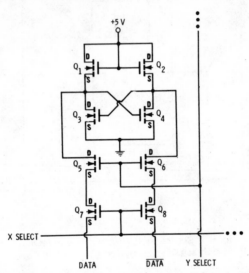

Fig. B-8. Static NMOS storage element (Signetics 2602).

CMOS and SOS Cells

CMOS devices are simply made of PMOS and NMOS inverters connected in series. If we tie the two drains together, an almost ideal complementary-symmetry inverter stage results. Such an ideal inverter is almost impossible to implement with npn/pnp pairs because neither device will turn completely off. Fig. B-9 shows the simplified CMOS stage and its cross section.

The basic CMOS storage element is much like earlier devices, in that two inverters are cross coupled to form the flip-flop. This is shown in Fig. B-10.

Storage cell selection and sensing of states are done by using PMOS transmission gates as shown in Fig. B-11. The p-channel transmission gates require a ground on the word line to select the desired cell.

CMOS memories exhibit all the characteristics of MOS flip-flops with some important extras, including very low power dissipation (milliwatts), low propagation delay, and high noise immunity. Actual storage cells require about six transistors per cell, and the actual cell area is much larger than equivalent PMOS and NMOS types.

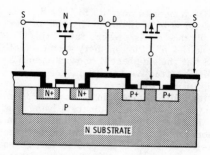

Fig. B-9. CMOS transistor schematic symbol and cross section.

Fig. B-10. CMOS storage element.

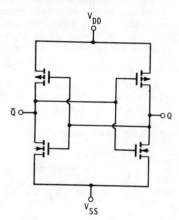

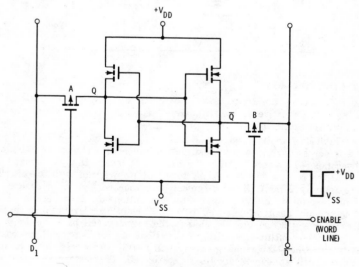

Fig. B-11. Six-transistor CMOS storage cell with
sense transmission gates A and B.

At present, CMOS memories have up to 1024 bits per chip. This figure will doubtlessly increase by a factor of 10, 100, or even 1000 if technology continues to advance at its present rate. Still, CMOS memories will lag behind the densities of other memory technologies due to the extra transistors. CMOS has the side benefit of working quite well in the linear mode, making CMOS attractive to system designers who want to combine linear and digital functions.

One problem with CMOS devices involves what is known as *parasitic conduction*. This is a result of a p substrate being near a p source and drain, and results in a breakdown and conduction. Such conduction paths require the additional step of creating isolation barriers in the manufacturing process. Moreover, there is the common MOS problem of parasitic capacitance resulting from a layer of silicon dioxide separating a metal gate and a conducting substrate. The only way to eliminate the capacitance is to reduce the substrate area, or start with another base for the substrate—such ideas have resulted in SOS technology, or Silicon On Sapphire. In SOS, the substrate-to-node capacitance is reduced, and therefore speed is increased as compared with CMOS.

Dynamic MOS Memory

The dynamic cell is a more simple structure than the static cell. Fig. B-12 shows a simple dynamic PMOS storage element. The figure shows that the presence or absence of *charge* on one of the flip-flop gates maintains a logic 1 or a logic 0 on the flip-flop output. How is this accomplished? MOS gates typically have an input impedance of 10^9 ohms in

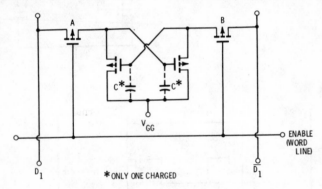

Fig. B-12. Dynamic MOS storage element.

parallel with a distributed capacitance of 2 pF. Because the capacitance is across such a large resistance, it can hold a charge for about 2 milliseconds. (This results from $t = RC$, which means that the charge on the gate for a logic 1 will leak off to 0.7 of its original logic 1 value in approximately 2 ms.) Since a typical processor with a cycle time of a few microseconds can execute many instructions in this period, some smart memory designer realized he could easily stop everything in the processor every 2 ms, quickly charge the memory cell back up (say in 1 μs) and then continue executing instructions. As far as overall processor time is concerned, the recharge delay will hardly be noticed, and the dynamic cell will appear to act like a static cell. Transistors are used on each flip-flop to sense and select one and only one cell. These are labeled A and B in Fig. B-12.

Even simpler cells than this can be constructed to operate in the dynamic mode. Fig. B-13 shows two *one*-transistor memory cells that rely on the capacitance (labeled C_s) that is distributed between the source and the substrate. Such small cells allow extremely high bit density on a chip. The following paragraphs describe the result of applying such a structure to make up a 4096-bit memory chip. The chip is produced by Texas Instruments and is called the TMS 4030. It is an amazing device packing over 4000 bits into a tiny 1-by-½-inch IC.

The MOS transistors used in the TMS 4030 are n channel and are used like transmission gates. When a logic 1 is written, the row and data/sense lines are raised to V_{DD} and C_s charges to V_{DD}. When data are being read, the row and data/sense lines are raised and sensed for logic 1 or 0.

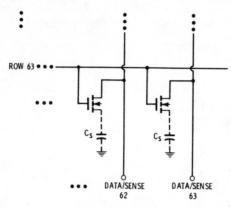

Fig. B-13. Two one-transistor dynamic MOS storage elements.

Fig. B-14 shows the structure of the TMS 4030 4K memory chip. When the chip enable input goes low (logic 0), an internal clock, with edge called ϕ_0, equalizes the voltages on the column inputs on either side of a "sense amplifier." Sixty-four of these differential sense amplifiers run across the center of the chip as illustrated, one for each column. Simultaneously, a voltage halfway between a logic 1 and a logic 0 is developed across a memory capacitor in an unused "dummy" bit row, of which there are two running on either side of the differential sense amplifiers. A pulse voltage generator circuit pumps charge to the dummy cells.

To refresh the memory, first an address is applied and the row decoders select one of 64 rows and the dummy bit row on the opposite side of the differential amplifier. (For a read, the above action occurs and one of the 64 columns is decoded. The charge on the cell at the selected row and the selected column is on one side of the differential amplifier, while the charge on the cell of the dummy row and the selected column is on the other side of the differential amplifier.) Since the dummy bits idle at one-half the supply voltage, the selected bits will be above or below this, i.e., a logic 1 or a logic 0, depending on the charge on C_s previously written. Now clock signal edge ϕ_0 occurs, and the differential sense amplifier latches into the sensed state. The states of the 64 bits in the selected row are now effectively restored. This is quite similar to the read/restore operation of magnetic core memory.

After the ϕ_0 clock edge, the column decoder passes the selected column into the column preamplifier. The selected logic 1 or logic 0 appears on

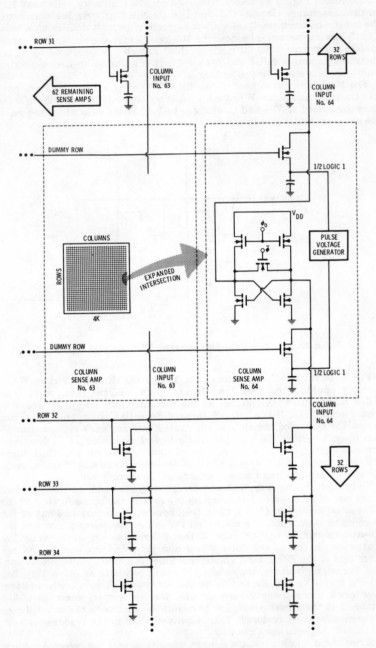

Fig. B-14. TMS 4030 4096-bit dynamic RAM.

the single data output lead. To write into memory, the column decode circuit selects one of the 64 columns to the "data-in" line. During the write, the sense amplifier on the selected column latches like a set/reset flip-flop, and new data are written into the row selected by the row decode address. The other bits on the row are simply refreshed during this write operation.

The complete block diagram of the memory chip is shown in Fig. B-15. This diagram shows how the simple cell structure forces a rather complex amount of peripheral circuitry. Yet, as far as external requirements are concerned, the device functions in a straightforward manner.

As far as updating is concerned, we need to refresh the row bits (i.e., addresses A_0–A_5) for 0.9 μs every 2 ms (a duty cycle of about 2000:1). A simple shift register can do the refreshing, cycling through the six addresses with a 1-MHz clock.

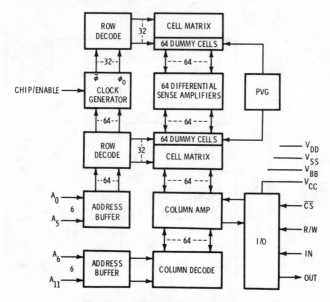

Fig. B-15. TMS 4030 block diagram.

READ-ONLY MEMORIES

The job of the ROM (Read-Only-Memory) cell is to permanently store a logic 1 or a logic 0. Such a simple function can be implemented in a number of ways, depending on the type of semiconductor material used.

Diode Matrix ROM

Perhaps the simplest example of a ROM memory is the diode matrix ROM shown in Fig. B-16. With the diodes connected as shown, addressing a bit requires raising the WORD line to logic 1 and grounding the DATA line. If a diode is connected at the selected row and column, the bit will be read as a logic 1 because the diode is forward-biased and provides a low-impedance current path to +5 volts through a cathode resistor. If no diode is connected, the output will be read as a logic 0 by a transistor pulling the row line to ground.

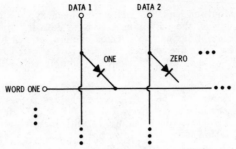

Fig. B-16. Diode connections in a ROM.

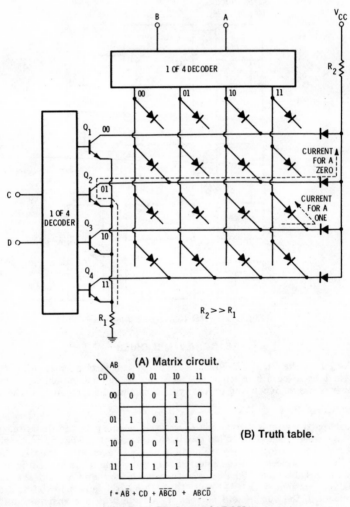

(A) Matrix circuit.

(B) Truth table.

$f = A\bar{B} + CD + \bar{A}\bar{B}\bar{C}D + ABC\bar{D}$

Fig. B-17. Diode matrix ROM.

Fig. B-17 shows how to make a simple 4-by-4 ROM memory using a diode matrix and TTL decoders. If we select a cell by applying a 4-bit address, a diode present at the junction of the selected row and column will provide a low-impedance current path to +5 volts, and a logic 1 will be read. If no diode is present (and R_2 is much greater than R_1), the output will be pulled low by a transistor (current path B) and a logic 0 will be read.

Note that we can easily remove the diodes with a soldering iron. In a way, then, we could say the diode ROM is "programmable." The 1's and 0's that are fixed by the diodes' positions can be reconfigured. Thus, we could call this ROM a PROM, or *Programmable ROM*. But, if the device is programmable (i.e., you *can* change the bit pattern), isn't it a RAM? The answer to this dilemma has to do with how we define "program-

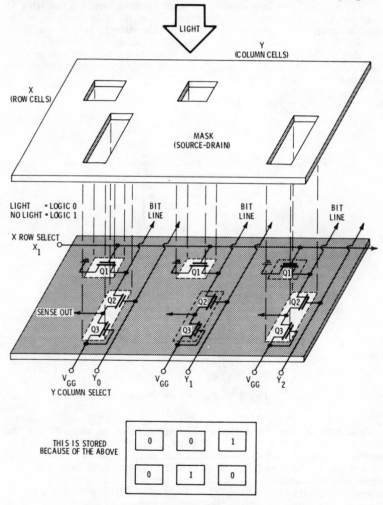

Fig. B-18. Mask programming a static ROM.

mable." In the memory industry, ROM cells are distinguished from PROM devices in that the ROM is an integrated circuit, usually programmed by the manufacturer, while the PROM is programmed by the user. Thus, the diode ROM is technically a PROM if we change the diodes, and only a ROM if we don't change the diodes. In large quantities, ROMs are "mask-programmed."

Mask-Programmed ROM

Consider a logic 1 to be stored at a permanent location in a memory matrix or cell location. A special template or mask is designed and reduced photographically to an extremely small size. The mask is made so that it allows light to expose only those cells that are to be logic 0's. Fig. B-18 shows the schematic symbol and masking operation for a MOS ROM cell. (Remember, this is occurring on a microscopic level.) Transistor Q_1 being accessible through the mask holes allows Q_1 to be included in the manufacturing diffusion process. Now when the memory chip is operating, and the bit or data line is sensed, or is taken to logic 0, a logic 0 will be read due to the inclusion of Q_1. On the other hand, no light through the mask over Q_1 will take Q_1 out of the circuit, and then raising the bit line will cause a logic 1 to be read.

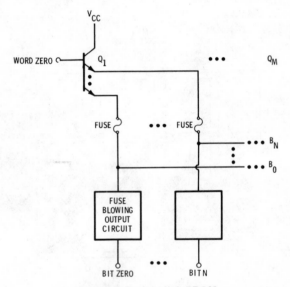

Fig. B-19. Fusible-link PROM.

Masked ROMs are organized in many sizes, from the small 32×8 size up to the large 2048×8. The code pattern for the ROM is supplied by the designer to the manufacturer. This code pattern will be in the form of 1's and 0's on either tabular boxed sheets of paper, 80-column computer cards, or computer paper tape. Often a higher-level language is used to develop the binary code, especially if the masked ROM is used in a micro-processor. Turnaround time is the main drawback of the masked ROM, usually running two to three weeks.

PROM Cells

As was pointed out, PROM cells do the same thing as ROM cells, with the exception that the user usually does the programming. There are two basic types of PROM: fusible-link, which can be written in only once and may not be changed later, and ultraviolet erasable (sometimes mistakenly called electrically alterable), which can be written in and erased many times.

Fusible-Link PROM

Fig. B-19 shows the fusible-link cell. Selecting a WORD enables one multiple-emitter word transistor, for example Q_1 in the figure. Each emitter is connected through a 200-angstrom–thick Nichrome fuse to the bit column. With all fuses intact, all bits are logic 0. To program a bit in a word, the word is addressed in the normal manner, and the bits of the

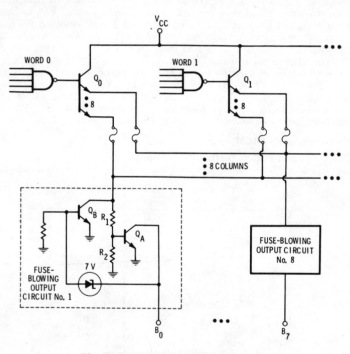

Fig. B-20. Fusible-link PROM (32 × 8).

word to be made a logic 1 are raised to a voltage that trips a comparator on the output pin. The comparator, in turn, directly grounds the selected emitter. Voltage V_{CC} is then raised above the normal +5 volts to +12.5 volts, which is enough to blow the respective fuse. Each bit of the word is programmed in this manner, until the entire word is complete. All circuits with blown fuses will be read as logic 1's during a read cycle.

There are other alternatives to using Nichrome fuses: polycrystalline silicon links (which don't suffer from a "grow back" condition) and back-to-back diodes.

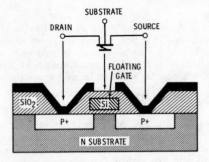

Fig. B-21. UVROM (FAMOS) inverter cell.

Fig. B-20 shows a typical fusible-link PROM memory IC organized as 32 words by 8 bits per word. The 32 words are implemented with 32 npn transistors with 8 emitters per transistor. Each emitter has a fuse in series with it. To program the PROM, a word is first selected via a five-input NAND gate, which turns on one of the transistors through R_1 in series with R_2. To store a logic 1 in the first bit of the eight-bit word, the respective output pin is raised to +8 volts. This breaks down the comparator zener diode, turning on Q_B and grounding one side of the fuse. The V_{cc} line is raised to +12.5 volts, which puts 4.5 volts across the fuse, causing it to blow open. The other 7 bits in the word, unless raised about the zener breakdown, effectively see the series resistance of $R_1 + R_2$, which keeps the current low enough to prevent the fuse from blowing.

Ultraviolet Erasable PROM

The need for a highly flexible PROM that could be used to develop and debug digital systems and microcomputers led to the development of the

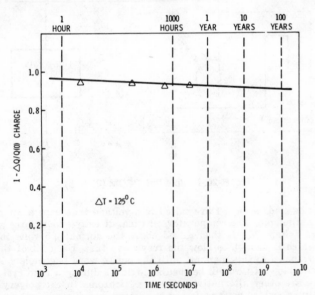

Fig. B-22. UVROM charge decay.

ultraviolet erasable PROM, or UVROM. This device is also called FAMOS for *F*ield *A*lterable *MOS*.

The UVROM cell, as shown in Fig. B-21, is similar in makeup to the standard PMOS cell, with the exception that the silicon gate is floating electrically from the source, drain, and substrate material. It is insulated by a thin layer of silicon dioxide.

A logic 1 is programmed into the cell by applying a high-voltage pulse between the source and drain of the cell. This causes an electron avalanche between these elements, which results in a buildup of negative charge on the floating gate. The charge will decay at an extremely slow rate, as Fig. B-22 shows.

Since the gate is negatively charged, the PMOS channel is enhanced, and a low resistance will exist between the source and drain. An extrapolation of the charge decay shows that this initial charge will drop less than 30% over 100 years.

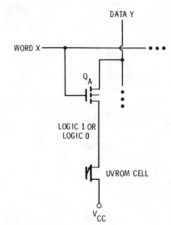

Fig. B-23. UVROM storage element.

Erasing the logic 1 is accomplished by bombarding the device with ultraviolet light. A quartz window on the chip allows the UV to enter. This results in the flow of photocurrent from the floating gate back to the substrate, thereby discharging the gate to its original state of non-conduction.

Fig. B-23 shows the basic UVROM memory cell. Once the *cell* is programmed to a logic 1 or 0, raising the WORD and DATA lines enables the cell state to appear through Q_A, causing either V_{CC} (logic zero) or V_{DD} (logic 1) to be read.

Fig. B-24A shows a single FAMOS cell along with its associated decoding, sensing, and programming circuits. Fig. B-24B shows how the 2048 cells in a UVROM chip are arranged in 8 planes of 8×32 cells. Each plane contains 256 FAMOS cells, located at the row/column intersects. The planes are stacked on top of each other, so that there are 8 bits (one on each plane) which share the same row/column intersect. This group of 8 bits can be treated as an 8-bit word being located at a specific (X, Y) coordinate.

To program a word, the address of the word (row/column intersect) is encoded on the address lines A_0–A_7. The bit pattern to be programmed is encoded on the D_0–D_7 data lines by grounding those bits which are to be

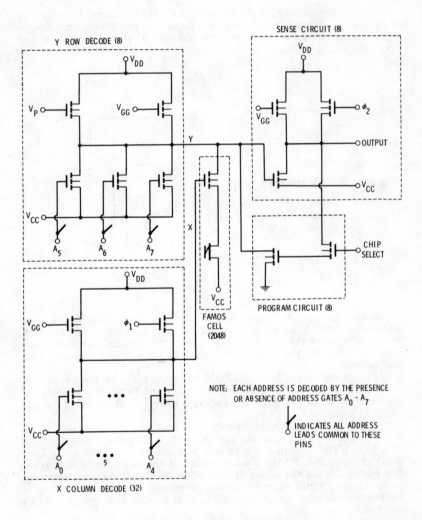

(A) FAMOS cell with associated circuitry.

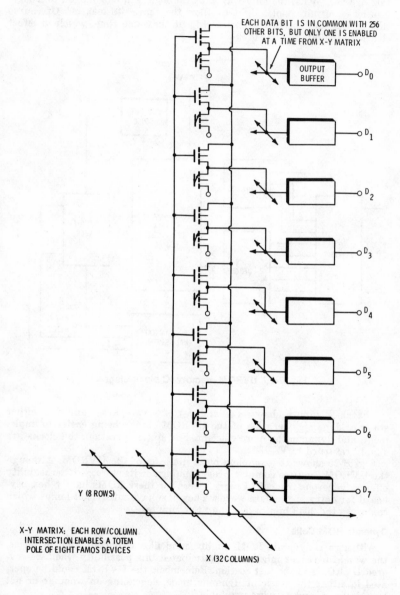

EACH DATA BIT IS IN COMMON WITH 256 OTHER BITS, BUT ONLY ONE IS ENABLED AT A TIME FROM X-Y MATRIX

OUTPUT BUFFER $\circ D_0$

$\circ D_1$

$\circ D_2$

$\circ D_3$

$\circ D_4$

$\circ D_5$

$\circ D_6$

$\circ D_7$

Y (8 ROWS)

X-Y MATRIX: EACH ROW/COLUMN INTERSECTION ENABLES A TOTEM POLE OF EIGHT FAMOS DEVICES

X (32 COLUMNS)

(B) Matrix of FAMOS cells in 2048-bit memory.

FAMOS cells.

programmed as logic 1, while setting the logic 0 lines at −40 volts. A −50-volt, 5-milliampere, 5-millisecond pulse is then applied to the V_{GG} and V_{DD} lines while V_{CC} is held at +12 volts. This will produce enough charge on the floating gate to turn it on, programming a logic 1. Once this has been done, the only way that the logic can be changed to a logic 0 is by using ultraviolet light to allow the charge to leak off. Of course this process is done to the entire chip at the same time, which in effect clears all the bits to logic 0.

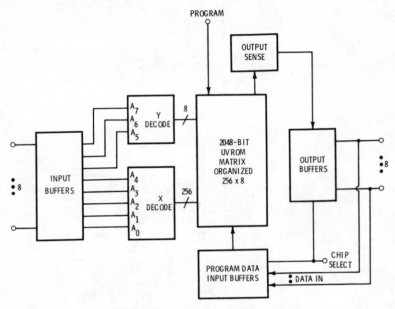

Fig. B-25. UVROM memory IC block diagram.

The clock inputs shown (ϕ_1 and ϕ_2) are two-phase, allowing either static or dynamic operation of the UVROM—static being easier to implement, and dynamic the more efficient. For static operation, the clocks are simply returned to V_{CC}.

Fig. B-25 shows the complete block diagram of the UVROM. Although the UVROM requires complex programming for its storage, its erasability offers a generous tradeoff. Programmers for these ROMs have a hex keyboard for entry of the data words. They also have ultraviolet lamps which can erase the 2048 bits in less than ten minutes.

Dynamic ROM Cells

Although a dynamic ROM might sound like a contradiction in terms, the watchful reader might have anticipated this possibility when we covered UVROMs in the last section. Remember, the UVROM could be operated in either the static or dynamic mode, depending on whether or not two clocks, ϕ_1 and ϕ_2, were available.

In essence, the dynamic ROM uses the same capacitor charge principle that is used in the dynamic RAM covered earlier, except that the bits are

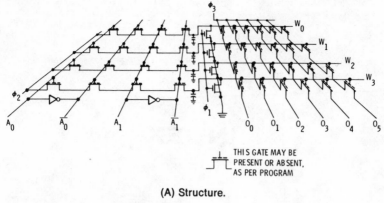

THIS GATE MAY BE
PRESENT OR ABSENT,
AS PER PROGRAM

(A) Structure.

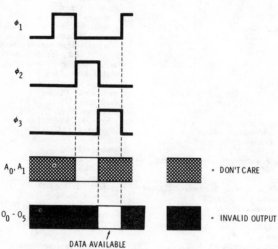

= DON'T CARE

= INVALID OUTPUT

DATA AVAILABLE

(B) Timing diagram.

Fig. B-26. Mask-programmed 4 × 6 dynamic ROM.

made either 1 or 0 by the absence or presence of physical gates on the chip.
Fig. B-26A shows a mask-programmed dynamic ROM, while Fig. B-26B
is a timing diagram for this simple memory. Such a ROM is rarely adver-
tised as being dynamic; however, careful examination of certain manufacturers' data sheets reveals that the clock must stay high to keep the
data from leaking off.

INDEX